Parting from the Four Attachments

Parting from the Four Attachments

*Jetsun Drakpa Gyaltsen's Song of Experience
on Mind Training and the View*

By Chogye Trichen Rinpoche

Commentary translated by Thubten Choedak

Root Text and Lineage Prayer translated by
H. H. Sakya Trizin and Jay Goldberg

Compiled and edited
by John Deweese

Snow Lion
Boston & London

Snow Lion
An imprint of Shambhala Publications, Inc.
Horticultural Hall
300 Massachusetts Avenue
Boston, Massachusetts 02115
www.shambhala.com

Printed in the United States of America

Designed and typeset by Gopa & Ted2, Inc.

Library of Congress Cataloging-in-Publication Data
Thub-bstan-legs-bśad-rgya-mtsho, Bco-brgyad Khri-chen XVIII,
1920–
Parting from the four attachments: Jetsun Drakpa Gyaltsen's song of
experience on mind training and the view / by Chogye Trichen Rinpoche; commentary translated by Thubten Choedak; root text and
lineage prayer translated by H.H. Sakya Trizin and Jay Goldberg;
compiled and edited by John Deweese.
p. cm.
Includes bibliographical references.
ISBN 978-1-55939-193-1 (alk. paper)
1. Spiritual life—Sa-skya-pa (Sect) 2. Sa-skya-pa (Sect)—
Doctrines. 3. Grags-pa-rgyal-mtshan, 1147–1216. Żen pa bźi bral
gyi man ṅag. I. Thubten Choedak. II. Ṅag-dbaṅ-kun-dga'-theg-
chen-dpal-'bar, Sa-skya Khri-'dzin, 1945– . III. Goldberg, Jay. IV.
Deweese, John, 1958– . V. Grags-pa-rgyal-mtshan, 1147–1216. Żen
pa bźi bral gyi man ṅag. English & Tibetan. VI. Title.
BQ7672.6.T48 2003
294.3'444—dc21
2003002033

Contents

Preface by His Holiness the Dalai Lama

───────────────── .♋ ─────────────────

FROM AMONG the vast and profound Dharma spoken by Vajradhara Chogye Trichen — "the great sage, treasure holder of the most secret Instructions for Disciples (*Lamdre Lobshe*)," incomparable in his kindness — that has been and continues to be taught by him throughout all the directions, on this occasion I am delighted and greatly rejoice in a compilation of the teachings given by this very Lord Protector on six occasions, concerning the guiding instructions and advice on Parting from the Four Attachments by the great and glorious Sakya master, the venerable Drakpa Gyaltsen.

I am very pleased that these teachings have been translated into English and are being published in the United States by Snow Lion Publications. I pray and make aspirations that on the basis of this, great benefit for all sentient beings will ensue; that many fortunate ones will easily gain perfect mental vision and the discernment to realize the true meaning of the teachings; and that all the wishes of this supreme and venerable lord and master, Chogye Trichen, may be spontaneously fulfilled.

This is written by the ordained follower of Buddha Shakyamuni, Tenzin Gyatso, who is known as the Dalai Lama, in the seventeenth sixty-year cycle, in the Water Horse year, on the tenth day of the third month, April 22, 2002.

Foreword by
Chökyi Nyima Rinpoche

THE EMINENT LORD of refuge and vajra holder Chogye Trichen is not only the hierarch of the illustrious great Sakyas' teachings of the ultimate lineage, his oceanlike mind is also the bearer of the empowerments, reading transmissions, and pith instructions belonging to the nonsectarian eight major chariots of the practice lineage. He is an esteemed vajra bearer of the triple precepts, a pure and learned lord of *siddhas*, and numerous sublime masters revere him at the crown of their heads and praise him unanimously, declaring that he is indeed a sublime great being.

Here is presented the great Jetsun Drakpa Gyaltsen's profound instruction on Parting from the Four Attachments, spoken in the form of a song of spiritual realization, together with a clarification by the eminent lord of refuge and vajra holder Chogye Trichen, whose gracious words are imbued with the resplendent warmth of blessings. While strewing flowers of applause upon this English translation, I add the wish that everyone in this wide world presently engaged in studies and reflections covering the classical works of Buddhism may enjoy the elixir of this pithy advice and that sublime blessings may infuse their stream of being.

This was written by Tulku Chökyi Nyima, who is counted among this master's disciples, on the auspicious tenth day of the third month, in the Tibetan year of 2129.

Acknowledgments

The teachings in this book are a compilation of six teachings on Jetsun Drakpa Gyaltsen's song of experience on Parting from the Four Attachments given by Chogye Trichen Rinpoche over the course of recent years. The first discourse was given during Chogye Rinpoche's 1996 visit to Canberra, Australia. The second teaching was given at Sakya Tenphel Ling, in Singapore, in 1998. The third occasion for these teachings was at a private meeting with Rinpoche in Kathmandu, Nepal, in 1999. The fourth teaching was given at La Sonnerie, in Dordogne, France, in 2000, at the request of Tulku Pema Wangyel. The fifth was in Adelaide, Australia, and the sixth in Brisbane, Australia, both in 2001. The Australian teachings were requested by Rinpoche's translator, Lama Thubten Choedak.

All of the teachings were recorded. The Australia and Singapore teachings were translated orally at the time of the teachings by Thubten Choedak. Those in France and Kathmandu were recorded at the time, and were orally translated and recorded on tape at a later date by Thubten Choedak. The oral translations were transcribed, compiled, and edited by John Deweese. With Chogye Rinpoche's permission, these teachings were supplemented by private oral instructions given over the years in Kathmandu, Nepal. These were recorded and carefully translated from the recordings by Guru Rinchen Chudar and John Deweese.

The root text of Drakpa Gyaltsen's song on Parting from the Four Attachments was translated by H. H. Sakya Trizin and Jay Goldberg and published in 1982 by Sakya Tenphel Ling, Singapore, in the volume *A Collection of Instructions on Parting From The Four Attachments*. This translation was very slightly edited by John Deweese, based on the commentary of Chogye Trichen Rinpoche and with reference to the Tibetan text and the translation by Cyrus Stearns. The lineage prayer by Ngorchen Kunga Zangpo was also translated by H. H. Sakya Trizin and Jay Goldberg and was published in the same volume.

The biography was compiled from the starting point of the few brief extant English biographies of Chogye Rinpoche, particularly that of Jay Goldberg, which was the product of his studies of Rinpoche's written autobiography, supplemented by details from interviews. The greater part of the biography is derived from extensive interviews conducted privately in Kathmandu, Nepal, in recent years. The contents of the biography are from Rinpoche himself or, in a few cases, from eyewitness accounts of those closest to him. All of the stories and material in the biography come from Chogye Rinpoche; all was duly recorded and remains in the archives of Jamchen Lhakang Monastery in Kathmandu, Nepal. The present version is part of a larger, more complete biography of Rinpoche currently under preparation by his disciples.

We wish to thank Jay Goldberg (Ngawang Samten Chophel) for his background work on Chogye Rinpoche's biography. David Jackson kindly sent us Jay Goldberg's short biography and allowed us to use some of the old photos of the lamas in Tibet that he has been able to collect over many years. We wish to thank the translator Venerable Matthieu Ricard for taking the time to read the manuscript and offer his comments. The translator Andreas Kretchmar carefully read the biography and commentary and also offered many excellent suggestions. Chogye Rinpoche's disciple and translator Cyrus Stearns was kind enough to give a detailed and thorough perusal of the entire manuscript and contributed many valuable insights and critical advice as well. Noellina Deweese carefully proofread the book and provided helpful editorial suggestions. Many thanks go to Sidney Piburn and Jeff Cox of Snow Lion Publications for supporting this project from the very beginning and patiently guiding us through the process of making a book. Many thanks also to Constance Miller, Daia Gerson, and Steve Rhodes of Snow Lion for their help in the editorial process. A note of appreciation is also due to Jeannette Nichols for her continuous support.

More information about Chogye Trichen Rinpoche may be found at Rinpoche's website, www.chogyetrichen.com.

A Brief Biography
of Jetsun Drakpa Gyaltsen

———— ✑ ————

JETSUN DRAKPA GYALTSEN (1147–1216) was the son of the great founding master of the Sakya tradition of Tibetan Buddhism, Sachen Kunga
Nyingpo (1092–1158), and younger brother of the renowned scholar
Sonam Tsemo (1142–82). Adopting the lifestyle of a reclusive meditator, he served his father, Sachen, who was also his main teacher, and
attained great realization. In his *History of the Sakya Tradition*, Chogye
Trichen Rinpoche gives the following short account of Drakpa Gyaltsen's life:

> Sonam Tsemo's younger brother Jetsun Drakpa was born in the Fire
> Hare year of the third cycle (1147). He had a great many teachers, the
> most important of whom were his father Sachen Kunga Nyingpo
> and his brother Sonam Tsemo. Endowed with the unceasing inspi-
> ration of Arya Manjushri, he displayed his profound view and vast
> activity which encompassed the teaching of the Tripitaka and all the
> tantras. He became a celebrated scholar, saint, and yogin who med-
> itated continually, who was capable of extinguishing all doubt con-
> cerning the profound meaning, and who possessed all the outer,
> inner, and secret signs of realization.
>
> When the famous Khache Panchen (1126–1225), who was skilled in
> astrology, announced that there was going to be an eclipse of the sun,
> Drakpa Gyaltsen let it be known that he was going to prevent this
> eclipse. In order to accomplish this, he stopped the movement of
> breath and mind in the right and left channels of the subtle body and
> caused the red and white "drops" to mix in the central channel of the
> subtle body. The eclipse was prevented by this yogic practice. The
> pandita declared that this was just a trick to make him look like a liar
> and went to visit Drakpa Gyaltsen. Upon his arrival, Drakpa Gyalt-

sen sprang to his feet and suspended his vajra and bell in midair. When he saw such signs that surpassed all understanding, Khache Panchen Shakya Shri exclaimed, "Great Vajradhara." Realizing that here was the most precious of all the vajra holders, he requested the nectar of his teaching.

When Drakpa Gyaltsen was fifty-six and living at the Nyemo Tsangkha Monastery, Sachen Kunga Nyingpo appeared and explained the Path and the Fruit to him. Drakpa Gyaltsen was able to bestow blessings by his very presence and had the power to transfer himself to different spiritual lands, although he had to decline when dakinis invited him to remain. Among his students there were eight whose names were suffixed by Drakpa, three who were great translators, four supreme students who held the teaching of the *Vajrapanjara*, and countless others such as Mon Vajra Raja.

He prophesied that when he was reborn as a chakravartin, a world-ruling emperor, in the Gold-Colored World, he would realize the majority of the levels and paths and would become a perfectly accomplished buddha after only three more incarnations.[1]

Jetsun Drakpa Gyaltsen exemplified the qualities of a genuine practitioner, as reflected in his many songs of spiritual realization, such as his song on Parting from the Four Attachments. He meticulously maintained the vows of ethical conduct while being both learned and realized in meditation practice. A fully accomplished *siddha* practitioner, he became one of the five great founding masters of the Sakya tradition of Tibetan Buddhism.

In his survey of the Sakya school and its broader context within the Buddhist tradition, entitled *A Waterdrop from the Glorious Sea*, the Sakya teacher Lama Sherab Gyaltsen Amipa presents a summary of the life of Jetsun Drakpa Gyaltsen:

> The third son of Kunga Nyingpo, Jetsun Rinpoche Drakpa Gyaltsen, took birth many times in the form of Indian and Tibetan mahapanditas, including the Indian *acharya* Gothayapa Lodro. After being a direct disciple of Manjushri for seven lifetimes, he took birth in Tocung as Lama Ngogton Bhughuwa, and at the age of eight, he received the *upasaka* vows from Jangsem Dagyal; but he did not sim-

ply remain an *upasaka*, for he also abstained from meat, alcohol, and eggs. His spiritual practice was no different from that of a true *bhik-shu*. Furthermore, all his primary followers were monks. He told them never to neglect their fortnightly confession, and he would serve them tea at that time. He took delight in those who had taken vows due to their aspiration for liberation, and he never broke even the least of his *pratimoksha*, bodhisattva, or tantric vows. His father, elder brother, and Nyan Tsugtor Gyalpo gave him the complete oral teachings on the sutras and tantras, and he gained an understanding of the world equal to that of Virupa. While practicing his sadhana, his vajra and bell would remain suspended in midair, and the bell would sound by itself. He could protect himself from the harms of the sun, moon, and Rahula and illustrated in many ways his attainment of *siddhi*s, his learning, and his dignity. Thus, the Kashmiri mahapandita Shakya Shri and the eight minor panditas who were his followers proclaimed, "Even in our land of the *aryas*, India, such a *siddha* as he is indeed rare."

In order to serve the followers of the Dharma in the future, he wrote the treatises: *The Celestial Tree of Clear Realization of the Groups of Tantras in General; The Pure Commentary on* The Two Examinations; *The Necklace Commentary; Written Guidance on* the Path and the Fruit; several commentaries on the Chakrasamvara Tantras and the Hevajra Tantras; *sadhana*s of Manjushri, Naropa's teaching on Vajrayogini, the twenty-one Taras, and Vajrakilaya; the text *Ray of Light Serving Others: A Meditational Practice of Vairochana;* and many others.

Among his innumerable disciples, four became famous; the greatest of these was Sakya Pandita. In brief, he found his only joy in Dharma, and it was widely known that when he died, he owned only one set of clothes. After devoting his life to immaculate service to the Dharma, he went to the divine realm of Sukhavati at the age of seventy.[2]

The instructions of Jetsun Drakpa Gyaltsen are the practical advice of one who has realized the truth of the Buddha's teachings through deep meditative experience. While his scholarly works are extensive, as shown above, Drakpa Gyaltsen is revered as a representative of the oral instruction lineage of realized meditators. His songs of meditative experience are not the lengthy explanations of a scholarly exponent of the written tradition. Rather, the teachings in the songs of experience of Drakpa Gyaltsen are what is known as *dam ngak*, or *men ngak*, experiential advice and key oral instructions. This is the tradition of instruction most valued by practitioners for revealing the central points and essential advice necessary to effectively practice and ultimately realize the teachings.

Drakpa Gyaltsen, like his father, Sachen Kunga Nyingpo, is part of a great tradition of realized meditators who impart these instructions, which includes such luminaries as the *mahasiddhas* of India and the great yogis of Tibet, such as the famed Milarepa. In his preface to *A Collection of Instructions on Parting From The Four Attachments*, published by Sakya Tenphel Ling, in Singapore, the American translator Jay Goldberg places these masters in the context of this stream of Buddhist teaching:

> The speech of Shakyamuni Buddha as presented in the collection of the *Tripitaka*, or *Three Baskets*, consists of instructions on moral conduct, meditation and wisdom. The eighty-four thousand different teachings included in this collection were taught for the sole purpose of destroying the poisonous afflictions of desire, hatred and delusion which bind living beings to this world of suffering. As these were spoken by the Enlightened One to help an individual or group overcome a specific problem hindering their path to ultimate happiness, the scriptures appear to be unsystematic and confusing.
>
> To clarify this and to put the teachings into a methodical system, two traditions arose among the great saintly luminaries who appeared after the Enlightened One. One tradition studied and understood the various scriptures and then wrote authoritative commentaries, known in Sanskrit as *shastra*, so that it would be easy for the followers on the path to liberation to progress through the various stages. Within this tradition are found great noble ones such as Nagarjuna, Asanga, Vasubandhu, Candrakirti, Shantideva, Buddhagosha, and the like. The second tradition was an oral tradition based on the realization of great masters. Due to a realization or certain understanding of the truth, the one who gained that realization

would pass down the method of entering the path and gaining the ultimate result to a disciple or group of disciples. Great saints, such as Virupa, Naropa, Atisha, or even the great Chan masters of China are included in this group. In Tibet also, among all the four main sects many great teachers have arisen to contribute to this tradition. One of them was the founding patriarch of the Sakya tradition, Sachen Kunga Nyingpo. At the age of twelve, through a direct realization of the Bodhisattva Manjushri, he received the teaching known as "*The Parting From The Four Attachments*" which brought him to a very profound understanding of the path to enlightenment. The teaching itself was only one verse of four lines, but its meaning included the entire path leading to Buddhahood.[3]

These observations, written about Drakpa Gyaltsen's father, Sachen Kunga Nyingpo, to whom the original teaching on Parting from the Four Attachments was revealed by the bodhisattva Manjushri, equally apply to Drakpa Gyaltsen himself. The words of his songs of realization are brief, but they embody in their most essentialized form all the teachings of the sutras and tantras of the Buddha. Thus, he represents a long tradition within Buddhism of those masters who condense the instructions of the Buddha into the key practical advice and guiding instructions necessary to practice the teachings and gain genuine realization of them.

NOTES

1. Chogay Trichen, *The History of the Sakya Tradition,* transls. Ven. Phende Rinpoche, Jamyang Khandro, and Jennifer Stott. Bristol, U.K.: Ganesha Press, 1983.

2. Sherab Gyaltsen Amipa, comp., *A Waterdrop from the Glorious Sea.* Rikon, Switzerland: Tibetan Institute.

3. H. H. Sakya Trizin and Ngawang Samten Chopel (Jay Goldberg), transls. *A Collection of Instructions on Parting From The Four Attachments.* Singapore: Sakya Tenphel Ling, 1982.

The Biography of
Chogye Trichen Rinpoche

⟨⟩

HIS EMINENCE Chogye Trichen Rinpoche, Ngawang Khyenrab Thubten Lekshay Gyatso, is the head of the Tsharpa school within the Sakya tradition of Tibetan Buddhism. The Sakya school has three principal subschools: the Sakyapa, founded by Sachen Kunga Nyingpo (1092–1158); the Ngorpa, founded by Ngorchen Kunga Zangpo (1382–1456); and the Tsharpa, founded by Tsarchen Losal Gyatso (1502–66).

The principal and most comprehensive teaching of the Sakya school is the Lamdre (pronounced "lamdray"). The term "Lamdre" means "the path (*lam*) with the result (*dre*)." Lamdre contains instructions and practices covering the whole range of both the sutra and the tantra teachings transmitted by Buddha Shakyamuni. It originated with Virupa, one of the Indian Buddhist *mahasiddha*s or "supremely accomplished ones." The central teachings and practices within the Lamdre are based on the scripture known as the *Hevajra Tantra*, the Vajrayana Buddhist tradition of the tantric deity Hevajra.

The Lamdre was brought to Tibet by the Tibetan translator Drogmi Lotsawa in the middle of the tenth century and was later codified in the twelfth century by Sachen Kunga Nyingpo. This teaching has been passed down through an unbroken lineage of masters right to the present day. During the time of the master Muchen Konchok Gyaltsen (1388–1469), the Lamdre was divided into two subtraditions: the uncommon Lobshe, or private explanation for close disciples, which emphasizies the oral instructions for meditation practice; and the more commonly given Tsogshe, the explanation for the general assembly.

The essence of the Lamdre is known as the view of the "inseparability of samsara and nirvana" (*khorde yerme*), which refers to the inseparability of worldly existence and enlightenment. There is no abandoning of samsara in order to achieve nirvana, as the mind is the root of both. Once mind has been understood to be the root of both, it follows that nirvana is just a transformation of samsara. Realizing this inseparability is the key to attaining enlightenment through the Lamdre teachings.

The Lamdre (the Path with the Result) is known as a vast, profound, and complete path to enlightenment. It is divided into two sections: the preliminary section and the tantric section. The preliminary section contains instructions and teachings of the Mahayana Buddhist tradition and focuses on the "three modes of appearance" or "three modes of perception" (*nang sum*), sometimes referred to simply as the "three visions": the impure perception, the perception of experience, and pure perception. The tantric section contains the esoteric teachings, especially the teachings on the "three tantras" or "three continuums" (*gyu sum*). In any generation, there are only a few lineage holders of the Lamdre within the Sakya tradition.

The Tsharpa branch of the Sakya school was founded by Tsharchen Losal Gyatso (1502–56), who established the Dar Drangmochen Monastery in Tsang Province in Tibet. Tsharchen was a master of extraordinary realization and beheld pure visions of Guru Padmasambhava, Vajrayogini, Chakrasamvara, Kalachakra, Yamantaka, and numerous other masters and tantric deities. He met them just as one would meet another person, face to face. The uncommon Path with the Result (*Lamdre Lobshe*) was transmitted and elaborated on by Tsarchen, as was the uncommon Vajrayogini practice lineage of the Skygoing Goddess of Naropa (*Naro Khachoma*).

The Tsharpa lineage is renowned for maintaining all the highly prized uncommon or most esoteric meditation lineages of the Sakya school, and thus, Tsharpa masters have been traditionally represented as the holders of the practice lineage within the Sakya tradition. The precious practice lineages for which the Tsharpa are known include the uncommon Path with the Result (*Lamdre Lobshe*), the uncommon Vajrayogini of Naropa, the greater and lesser Mahakala, the Thirteen Golden Dharmas, the Kalachakra of the Jonangpas, and many others.

The lineage holder Chogye Trichen Rinpoche is the twenty-sixth patriarch of Phenpo Nalendra Monastery and is the head lama of the Tsharpa branch of the Sakya school. At present Rinpoche resides in Kathmandu, Nepal. Phenpo Nalendra is one of the main monasteries of the Tsharpa tradition, located in the Phenyul Valley just northeast of Lhasa in central Tibet. It was founded in 1435 by one of the great masters in the history of the Sakya tradition, Rongton Sheja Kunrig (1367–1449). Nalendra is one of the most important Sakya monasteries, with branch monasteries throughout Tibet. Named after that incomparable center of classical Buddhist learning, Nalanda Monastery in Bihar, India, during its first twenty years Nalendra grew to house 3,000 monks. Over the course of more than 500 years, Phenpo Nalendra generally had between 700 and 1,000 resident monks, as well as being home to thousands of visiting monks studying at the colleges there. There were many branch monasteries in various parts of Tibet, from Tsang to Amdo.

Famed as a stronghold of the esoteric practice lineage within the Sakya tradition, Nalendra became the principal monastery of the Tsharpa branch of the Sakya school, due to the extraordinary masters of the practice lineage who were its throne holders. It was also a repository of the teachings of all the eight great practice lineages of Tibet and thus was a center of the broader, nonsectarian approach to Buddhist practice. As just one recent example of this, the previous Chogye Trichen, throne holder of Nalendra, was a close disciple of the Fifteenth Karmapa, Khakyab Dorje, receiving in particular many teachings in the tradition of the Great Perfection (*dzogpa chenpo*), such as the Precious Collection of Revealed Treasures (*Rinchen Terdzod*).

Great meditators from all branches of the Sakya school went to Nalendra Monastery for practice and retreat. In modern times, prior to 1959, they came to train in the practice of retreat at Nalendra as disciples of Dampa Rinpoche, Zhenpen Nyingpo, of Ngor, Zimog Rinpoche of Nalendra, and Chogye Trichen Rinpoche. There were many retreat centers in the surrounding mountains, including two special hermitages where yogis remained in lifetime retreat. Whenever one of these yogis passed away, the event was inevitably accompanied by the appearance of rainbows, miraculous signs, and wonders. A monk who came out of Tibet with Chogye Rinpoche remarked that this was so commonplace that the monks would say, "Well, of course he had signs, he stayed in lifelong retreat!"

Nalendra was one of the most renowned centers in all of Tibet for the practice of the female tantric deity Vajrayogini. There were said to be generation after generation of yogis who, through the practice of Vajrayogini in the form of Naro Khachoma, accomplished the fruition of "going to the celestial realms" (*khacho*). Through Vajrayogini, they were able to transfer to the paradise of Khechara, the Akanishta pure realm of the *sambhogakaya* buddha-fields.

Some dissolved their physical bodies into rainbow light at the time of death. Some left this world with their physical bodies and accompanied Vajrayogini into the sky, disappearing into space as they journeyed to her pure realm. Some met her while moving among people and departed with her to the Khechara pure land; and for some, her coral staircase appeared in their meditation rooms, and they ascended to Vajrayogini's pure land. Many of the Chogye Trichen Rinpoches displayed the signs of Khechara. The previous Chogye Trichen, Rinchen Khyentse Wangpo (1869–1927), manifested signs of *phowa*, the transference of consciousness, to Vajrayogini's paradise at the time of his passing from this world.

The founder of Nalendra monastery, Rongton Sheja Kunrig (1367–1449), also known as Kunkhyen Rongtongpa, was born in eastern Tibet in Gyalmo Rong. Based on prophecies, as well as on his activities, Rongton was regarded as an emanation of Maitreya, the next buddha of our fortunate eon. His earlier incarnations included the Indian *acharya* Haribhadra and the pandita Kamalashila. He became known as one of the "six gems of the Sakya tradition" in recognition of his unparalleled mastery of the sutra tradition in general and the scriptures of Prajñaparamitaand the teachings of Maitreya in particular. The present Chogye Trichen received Rongton's teachings on the Prajñaparamita from the great bodhisattva Khunu Lama Tenzin Gyaltsen, as well as from other masters.

Rongton wrote three hundred works, ranging from eulogies to philosophical treatises to commentaries on the tantras. He was known to have realized at the very least the sixth bodhisattva level of spiritual attainment (*bhumi*), and it is said that he realized the truth of the nature of reality (*dharmata*). According to his biographies, Rongton could send forth multiple emanations of himself, resurrect deceased beings, and fly in space. As he entered the higher stages of realization, he became more and more childlike. He had liberated conceptual thinking and so behaved and spoke with the innocence of a child. He was a great bodhisattva and a great tantric master.

A contemporary of Tsongkhapa, founder of the Gelug school, Rongton was the first to challenge the Gelug philosophical teachings, and his students Gorampa and Shakya Chogden composed penetrating refutations of Tsongkhapa's interpretation of Madhyamaka. Nonetheless, Tsongkhapa held Rongton in the highest esteem, revealing to his student Khedrup-je that he regarded Rongton as none other than the bodhisattva Maitreya.

At the age of eighty-four, Rongton announced that he was to depart for the Tushita heaven, where the bodhisattva Maitreya dwells. A few days later he passed away, dissolving into Maitreya. Rongton manifested one of the varieties of rainbow body at his passing whereby the physical body dissolves into a body of rainbow light. His body shrank to a very small size and became extremely light in weight, but before it completely disappeared, it suddenly stopped shrinking and turned into a jewel relic, becoming again somewhat heavier. The tradition is that his fruition of a rainbow body was probably a result of the practice of Vajrayogini, even though as a manifestation of bodhisattva Maitreya himself, many means of manifesting the rainbow body were available to him.

Following the initial era of its founding, some misfortunes and outbreaks of illness had befallen Nalendra monastery. In response, the twenty-first Sakya throne holder, Dagchen Lodro Gyaltsen (1444–95), determined that the abbot and throne holder of the monastery should not be solely a great tantric adept but should also be one who had attained the level of a bodhisattva in accordance with the Mahayana Buddhist vehicle. Thus, Khyenrab Choje (1436–97) of the Zhalu Kushang branch of the ancient Che family was installed as the throne holder and eighth abbot of the monastery. Khyenrab Choje has been succeeded by seventeen holders of the Chogye Trichen title, all of whom have come from the Che family, from his "bone lineage" of patrilineal descent. From the time of Khyenrab Choje until the Chinese invasion of Tibet, Nalendra suffered no more obstacles.

The Nalendra throne holder's title, Chogye Trichen, is composed of two terms: *chogye*, "eighteen"; and *trichen*, "throne holder." It is said that the name Chogye is derived from the time of Khyenrab Choje, the first holder of the throne at Nalendra to come from the Zhalu Kushang family. Khyenrab Choje was invited by the Chinese emperor to come to China, but was unable to go, and so he sent his nephew, Jamyang Donyo Gyaltsen, as his representative. Through this nephew, the emperor bestowed the title of Chogye Trichen on the throne holder of Nalendra, lauding eighteen (*chogye*) exalted spiritual qualities he wished to recognize in Khyenrab Choje. The "eighteen" in this title also alludes to the date in the lunar calendar that celebrates the anniversary of Khyenrab Choje.

The Chogye Trichens received many offerings from the Chinese emperors. One unique offering was the ceremonial hat, a copy of which Chogye Rinpoche is often seen wearing in photos. This hat is replete with symbolism of Vajrayana Buddhism in general and of the deity Hevajra in particular. The famous hat was named "only ornament of the world" by the emperor. Subsequent holders of the throne of the Chogye Trichen continued to receive many honors from the Chinese emperors.

While in meditation retreat in the Potala in Lhasa, as a result of his spiritual practice, Khyenrab Choje beheld the sustained vision of the female tantric deity Vajrayogini against the backdrop of the cliffs of Drak Yerpa and received extensive teachings and initiations directly from her. Two forms of Vajrayogini appeared out of the face of the rocks at Drak Yerpa, one red in color and the other white, and together they bestowed the Kalachakra initiation on Khyenrab Choje. When asked if there was any proof of this, his attendant showed the kusha grass Khyenrab Choje had brought back with him from the initiation. It was unlike any kusha grass found in this world, with rainbow lights sparkling up and down the length of the dried blades of grass. This direct lineage from Vajrayogini is the shortest, the most recent, and the most direct lineage of Kalachakra that exists in this world. In addition to being known as an emanation of Manjushri, Khyenrab Choje had previously been born as many of the Rigden kings of Shambhala as well as numerous Buddhist masters of India. These are some indications of his unique relationship to the Kalachakra tradition.

Since the time of Khyenrab Choje, all the Chogye Trichens have come from the Zhalu Kushang branch of the Che family, so the lineage of the Chogye Trichens has been of patrilineal descent, held by descendants of the "bone lineage" of the Kushang family. The ongoing emanation of bodhisattvas through the "bone lineage" is found in some traditions of Tibetan Buddhism, and "bone lineage" emanations are very highly respected for many reasons. This is particularly so when the family is originally descended from the celestial gods. In this regard, the Che family shares a similar history with the Khon family of H. H. Sakya Trizin, as the story of both families begins with the original descent of the gods of clear light (*prabhashvara-devas*) into our world. The present Chogye Trichen, Ngawang Khyenrab Lekshay Gyatso, is the eighteenth Nalendra throne holder in the lineage beginning with Khyenrab Choje to have come from the Zhalu Kushang family.

In her *Great Commentary on Chod*, the famed female master Machig Lapdron prophesied three future emanations of Maitreya who would appear in Rongton's lineage, each of whose names would contain the word *khyen* or "knowledgeable." These are Khyenrab Choje (1438–97), Khyenrab Jampa (1633–1703), and Rinchen Khyentse Wangpo (1869–1927). All three held the title of Chogye Trichen, throne holder of Nalendra Monastery. Rinchen Khyentse Wangpo, the third Maitreya incarnation prophesied by Machig Lapdron, was the last Chogye Trichen before the present throne holder, Khyenrab Lekshay Gyatso, who is also the nephew of Rinchen Khyentse Wangpo. Chogye Rinpoche has consecrated a twelve-meter statue of Maitreya at his monastery in Bouddhanath, Nepal, maintaining the tradition of the blessings of his lineage that come down through the *khyen* incarnations of Maitreya.

The present Chogye Trichen Rinpoche is the eldest lama of the Sakya school of Tibetan Buddhism. Rinpoche was born into the blessed Che clan, a lineage said to have descended from the Clear Light Gods. Chogye Trichen Rinpoche is the scion and venerated elder of the Zhalu Kushang branch of the Che clan. Members of the Che clan entered the Buddhist path even before the time of the Tibetan king Songtsen Gampo in the early seventh century and were among the disciples of Guru Padmasambhava.

Remarkably, each generation of the Kushang family has produced not less than four sons, the majority of whom took their places as throne holders of many important monasteries, including Nalendra,

Zhalu, and Ngor. The name *Kushang* means "royal maternal uncle," deriving from the fact that many daughters of the family were married to numerous throne holders of the Sakya Khon family. This inter-marriage with the Khon family began in the Sakya or Yuan period (thirteenth to fourteenth century). At this time, one of the daughters of the Kushang family married Drogon Chagna, the brother of Chogyal Phagpa, who ruled Tibet following Chogyal Phagpa.

Many *heruka*s, some of whom were manifestations of the tantric deity Hevajra, have been born into the Che family. The masters of the Che family, including the present Chogye Trichen, often have a special birthmark, markings resembling tiger stripes on the thighs, like the tigerskin skirt of *heruka*s such as Hevajra and Kalachakra. Chetsun Senge Wangchuk, the early *dzogchen* master who attained the rainbow body of the great transference, is the patrilineal, or "bone-lineage" ancestor of Chogye Trichen Rinpoche. Since the time of Chetsun Senge Wangchuk in the eleventh to twelfth century, the Che family, as hold-ers of the practice lineages of Tibetan Buddhism, has produced count-less *siddha*s (fully accomplished practitioners) down to the present day.

The present Chogye Trichen Rinpoche, Khyenrab Lekshay Gyatso, was born in 1919 near Gyashar Kushang Monastery in Shigatse, in the Tsang Province of central Tibet. His father was Sonam Senge Wang-chuk (1873–1928) and his mother was Chime Drolkar (1895– ca.1963), also known as Namdrol Yeshe Sangmo, a daughter of the Shukhupa family of Nar Peling, a monastic estate of the Thartse Labrang of the Ngor school of the Sakya tradition.

From the age of four to the age of seven, Rinpoche journeyed on pilgrimage with his parents, reaching as far as Mount Kailash in the west-ernmost part of Tibet. Rinpoche's parents were accomplished practi-tioners of the teachings of the Great Perfection (*dzogpa chenpo*). Their principal root guru was De Gya Rinpoche, a close disciple of the cele-brated Nyingma master Dudjom Lingpa. At the time that Chogye Rin-poche was on pilgrimage with his parents, De Gya Rinpoche was dwelling in western Tibet. He bestowed many teachings and blessings on Chogye Rinpoche and his parents and made predictions regarding them.

De Gya Rinpoche offered Rinpoche and his parents a letter con-taining verses of blessing, which said, "May Sonam Senge Wangchuk realize the view of Dzogpa Chenpo. May Namdrol Yeshe Sangmo per-

fect the four visions. May the activities of Tsering Namgyal Dorje
[Chogye Rinpoche] be equal to the sky." Chogye Rinpoche explains
that this letter is a blessing and a prediction that his father would attain
realization through the *dzogchen* practice of the view of "cutting
through" (*trek chod*), that his mother would attain realization through
the *dzogchen* practice of perfecting the four visions of the "direct crossing" (*thogal*), and that Rinpoche himself would perform activities that
would spread far and wide.

Chogye Rinpoche's parents were surprised by the declarations of De
Gya Rinpoche's letter of blessing, since their young son had not been
recognized as a *tulku* or chosen as a lama. When they returned to central Tibet, and their son was subsequently selected as the Chogye
Trichen, their faith in De Gya Rinpoche greatly increased. Chogye Rinpoche also has great faith in De Gya Rinpoche. It seems that each of
his blessings has come true.

Chogye Rinpoche's father, Sonam Senge Wangchuk, was a great yogi
who practiced meditation day and night. Before he passed away, he sat
upright in meditation posture for two weeks in a kind of meditation
state (*tukdam*) entered by yogis prior to physical death. During this
two-week period it sometimes seemed that he might have already
passed away, but then he would speak again. When finally he passed,
his body was taken to the top of the family residence, and many rainbows appeared as it was burned. These signs were witnessed by many
people, including Chogye Rinpoche's brother and uncle.

Rinpoche has said that while his father must have been a great practitioner, his mother was greater. Whereas Rinpoche's father mainly
practiced Dzogchen *trek chod*, the wisdom practice of primordial
purity, his mother persevered in Dzogchen *thogal*, the visionary practice of spontaneous presence, the fruition of which is said to be superior to that of *trek chod*. Chogye Rinpoche speaks of his mother with
the deepest respect, admiration, love, and affection. Rinpoche feels that
she must have been a bodhisattva. She would never speak ill of anyone, and whenever someone was criticized, she would rush to their
defense, insisting that they could never do or say whatever they were
accused of. She was a great yogini, a twenty-four-hour-a-day practitioner of meditation.

Chogye Rinpoche's sister, Kunzang Tendrol, mentions that their mother would remain sitting upright in meditation throughout the night, and that she never dozed off for more than five or ten minutes at a time, all the while sitting upright. The family appreciated this, as no one had to worry about getting up at night to stir the fire ashes so that they would be ready for preparation of morning tea! The day she passed away, she was lying with her head in Chogye Rinpoche's lap. She said to Rinpoche that she was so happy and at peace that day, resting there in her son's lap. Then she closed her eyes and passed away.

Between the ages of seven and eight, Chogye Rinpoche lived at Shangpo Hermitage, where his father and elder brother taught him reading and writing. At that time, Rinpoche also memorized the text *Reciting the Names of Manjushri (Manjushri-namasamgiti)*, an essential work of tantric Buddhism. As a young person, Rinpoche wished to devote his time to study, contemplation, and meditation.

In 1928, at the age of nine, Chogye Trichen Rinpoche received a letter from the Thirteenth Dalai Lama Thubten Gyatso (1876–1933), recognizing him as the Eighteenth Chogye Trichen of the Phenpo Nalendra Monastery in central Tibet. In a subsequent letter, as well as in conversation when Chogye Rinpoche received novice monastic ordination from the Thirteenth Dalai Lama, the Dalai Lama referred to Rinpoche as the "Chogye Incarnate Lama."

The disciples of the previous Chogye Trichen, Rinchen Khyentse Wangpo (ca.1869–1927) understood this to mean that Rinpoche was both the reincarnation of the previous Chogye Trichen and the holder of the previous Chogye Trichen's "bone lineage." This would be quite unusual, since the present Chogye Trichen was already eight years old when Rinchen Khyentse Wangpo passed away. However, such circumstances are occasionally found in the biographies of great masters. The previous Chogye Trichen, Rinchen Khyentse Wangpo, was similarly mentioned in a letter from the Twelfth Dalai Lama to be both the reincarnation and the bone lineage emanation of Khyenrab Choje and other great holders of the Nalendra throne.

In 1929, at the age of ten, Chogye Rinpoche received the vows of a novice monk and was officially enthroned at the Nalendra Monastery. His tutor was Champa Kunga Chophel. During his first few years at Nalendra, Rinpoche completed retreats of Vajrapani, Hayagriva, and Manjushri. In his mid-teenage years, Chogye Rinpoche invited Lama

Ngawang Lodro Rinchen (ca.1892–1959), also known as Lama Ngaglo Rinpoche, to stay in the room beside his, where he remained for the next eight or ten years. Ngalo Rinpoche was the disciple of the previous Chogye Trichen, Rinchen Khyentse Wangpo, as well as the disciple of Zimog Rinpoche. Ngaglo Rinpoche was also a non-sectarian (*rime*) master who studied extensively with many masters of other schools and passed these traditions on to Chogye Trichen Rinpoche.

During this period, the highly accomplished scholar and yogi Lama Ngaglo transmitted all the traditions of classical Buddhist scholarship to Chogye Rinpoche. He also transmitted and trained Rinpoche in all the practices of Vajrayana Buddhist meditation. For two or three years, when Chogye Rinpoche was ages fifteen to eighteen, Lama Ngaglo trained him in the tantric yogas of the subtle channels (*nadi*) and vital winds (*prana*) as well as the yogic physical exercises (*trulkor*).

From his enthronement until the age of thirty-nine, Chogye Rinpoche remained at Nalendra Monastery, where he mastered the monastic scriptural rituals, the rituals of mandala, the ritual musical accompaniment, as well as the major meditation practice lineages of Tibetan Buddhism. To this day, Rinpoche maintains full monastic (*bhikshu*) ordination, and he is renowned for the purity with which he upholds the *pratimoksha* vows of the Buddhist monastic code (*Vinaya*). In addition, Rinpoche fully maintains all the bodhisattva precepts and the tantric commitments (*samaya*). Thus, he is distinguished as one of those rare masters who flawlessly upholds all three sets of vows of the three Buddhist vehicles: the *pratimoksha* vows of the vehicle of individual liberation (Hinayana), the bodhisattva vows of the great vehicle (Mahayana), and the tantric commitments of the diamond vehicle (Vajrayana).

Chogye Rinpoche has completed meditation retreats of all the major deities of the four classes of Buddhist tantra. During his late teens he carried out retreats of the tantric deities Guhyasamaja, Mahakala, Singhamukha, White Manjushri, and White Tara. Rinpoche pursued extensive studies of all major fields of knowledge taught in the Buddhist tradition. He is a scholar of literature, poetry, history, and Buddhist metaphysics and an accomplished master of traditional Tibetan poetry. He studied various branches of the literary arts under several distinguished experts. Very fond of poetry, Rinpoche wrote a detailed commentary on the Tibetan translation of Dandin's Sanskrit manual of classical poetics.

Chogye Rinpoche's principal root gurus are the Fifth Zimog Tulku, Ngawang Tenzin Thrinley (1884–1963), and Dampa Rinpoche, Zhenpen Nyingpo (1876–1952), abbot of Ngor Evam Monastery, who is also the principal root guru of H. H. Sakya Trizin. Dampa Rinpoche is from the ancient Nub family and is a descendant of Namkhai Nyingpo, the famed disciple of Guru Padmasambhava. The Zimog Rinpoches are the other throne holders at Nalendra Monastery, in addition to the Chogye Trichens. From his two principal root teachers, Chogye Rinpoche received innumerable initiations, transmissions, oral instructions, and ritual traditions of all classes of Buddhist tantra. In 1937, at the age of eighteen, Chogye Rinpoche went on pilgrimage with his mother for two years. During this time, he received from Dampa Rinpoche, at the monastery of Tanak Thubten in Tsang, the Collection of Tantras (*Gyude Kuntu*), which includes initiations and teachings from the Lamdre.

In addition to Chogye Rinpoche's main gurus, there were eight accomplished *siddha* monks at Nalendra Monastery with whom Rinpoche studied. There were never less than twenty monks in strict Vajrayana meditation retreat at Nalendra at any given time over the centuries. There were four great tantric temples dedicated to the four great tantric deities practiced at Nalendra. Only those monks who had fulfilled all the retreat commitments of a specific deity were allowed to participate in the rituals at the particular temple devoted to that deity. Through many such means, the practitioners at Nalendra were able to maintain an extraordinary level of spiritual commitment (*samaya*) and accomplishment over the course of many centuries.

Dampa Rinpoche, Zhenpen Nyingpo, was a rare and extraordinary master, one of the central masters of his time. Chogye Rinpoche has said that he considers Dampa Rinpoche to have the same qualities as the greatest lamas of the previous generation, such as Jamyang Khyentse Wangpo, Jamgon Kongtrul, and Jamyang Loter Wangpo. Rinpoche describes the blessing power of Dampa Rinpoche as being unique among the many lamas from whom he received initiation. When Dampa Rinpoche would give Vajrayana initiations, wonderful signs would arise at the time of the descent of the blessings of primordial wisdom (*yeshe bab*). Some disciples would shake, cry, or display various affects. Then Dampa Rinpoche would give the pointing-out instruction, admonishing them to recognize the nature of their minds.

When Chogye Rinpoche was receiving the Gyude Kuntu from Dampa Rinpoche, these kinds of signs of blessing occurred consistently. For example, there was one monk, a student of Dampa Rinpoche, who had one bad eye. He would sit very upright, maintaining the proper posture of meditation. During initiations, during the descent of blessings, he would often levitate off the ground, all the while maintaining his meditation posture. Those sitting around him would wait for this to occur, and sometimes they would slide his meditation cushion out from under him, then push it back again, to the awe and amusement of everyone present!

Chogye Rinpoche recounts a story told by Dampa Rinpoche about one of his retreats. One time, while he was doing the retreat of the meditation deity Vajrabhairava, Dampa Rinpoche visualized himself in the form of Vajrabhairava, enormous in size, his head reaching all the way up to the Heaven of the Thirty-three Gods that rule our universe. From there he looked down at the worlds of samsara below, and in the western direction he beheld the realms of the hells. In his form as Vajrabhairava, Dampa Rinpoche gave a kick at the hell realms, and instantly all the beings he had seen there just a moment before disappeared! This story may be understood as an example of the ability of bodhisattvas to liberate sentient beings through the power of the meditation deities.

Chogye Rinpoche's other root guru is Zimog Tulku Ngawang Tenzin Thrinley, who passed away in 1963. Zimog Rinpoche was quite jovial and lighthearted. He used to joke with his attendants with such informality that they felt comfortable joking with Rinpoche in return. He always appeared to be very happy. This joyous and humorous attitude is said to give a long life, and Chogye Rinpoche feels this is why Zimog Rinpoche lived to the age of eighty. Rinpoche also mentions that Dampa Rinpoche, on the other hand, did not joke around and appeared quite powerful and dignified. Zimog Rinpoche spent a great deal of time in meditation retreat.

Zimog Rinpoche's principal root master from the Sakya tradition was the previous Chogye Trichen, Rinchen Khyentse Wangpo. In addition to being the lineage holder of all the precious Sakya teachings, Zimog Rinpoche was a great non-sectarian (*rime*) lama who was diligent in seeking out gurus from the other schools of Tibetan Buddhism and receiving all of their teachings. From the Nyingma tradition, his main guru was Chusang Rinpoche, one of the two throne holders of the monastery of Dorje Drak in central Tibet. He received and studied all the traditions of the Kagyu tradition from the previous Dabsang Rinpoche, including the Hundred Teachings of the Jonangpas. He also received many teachings from Gelug masters.

In 1939, at the age of twenty, Chogye Rinpoche returned from pilgrimage and entered a nine-month retreat on the meditation deity Hevajra at Nalendra Monastery. Two years later, in 1941, Rinpoche bestowed the Hevajra teachings, the uncommon Path with the Result (*Lamdre Lobshe*), which he had received from his guru, Zimog Rinpoche. Only twenty-two years old at the time, Rinpoche imparted the teachings to 150 monks and others who had gathered at Nalendra. The following year Rinpoche gave the common Path with the Result (*Lamdre Tsogshe*) to 100 monks and additional disciples.

Following this, Chogye Rinpoche went into meditation retreat on the female tantric deity Vajrayogini in the form known as Naro Khachoma. Over the next few years, he intensively studied classical Buddhist texts, such as those of the Abhidharma, under his teacher, the Nalendra *khenpo* (abbot) Lama Ngaglo Rinpoche. Following this, Chogye Rinpoche wished to enter a longer period of meditation training, and he performed retreats of the meditation deities Maha Vairochana, White Tara, and the special Tsharpa tradition of Yamantaka.

During this period, Chogye Rinpoche received further detailed teachings on the Lamdre Lobshe from Zimog Rinpoche. Then he entered retreat on the deity Vajrakilaya. Soon after, Rinpoche completed another retreat, this time of the great tantric deity Kalachakra, following which he bestowed the Kalachakra initiation on 6,000 disciples at Nalendra Monastery. This was followed by retreats on Manjushri, Avalokiteshvara, and Vajrapani in one mandala, and on the protector Chaturmukha.

Chogye Rinpoche has received rare and precious teachings and "whispered instructions" from some of the great masters of modern

times, such as Dzongsar Khyentse Jamyang Chokyi Lodro (1893–1959).
He received teachings from Khyentse Chokyi Lodro during two or
three of his visits to Lhasa and central Tibet. From Khyentse Chokyi
Lodro, Chogye Rinpoche received the Nyingthig Yabzhi and many
other teachings of the Dzogchen Nyingthig, such as the "mind treasures" (*gong ter*) of the great leader of the non-sectarian (*rime*) movement, Jamyang Khyentse Wangpo (1820–92). Rinpoche also received
"whispered instructions" of the Sakya practice lineages such as the Path
with the Result from Khyentse Chokyi Lodro. One of these visits took
place in 1956, when Chogye Rinpoche was thirty-seven. In the autumn
of that year Rinpoche again bestowed the Lamdre Lobshe and then
entered a retreat of Chakrasamvara.

In the face of the Communist invasion of Tibet in 1959, Chogye Rinpoche, together with a party of thirty-two that included his guru,
Zimog Rinpoche, his mother, and the elderly Tsetrul Rinpoche of Nalendra, made his way to the safe haven of Lo Monthang, in Mustang in
northwestern Nepal. They traveled slowly, taking three months to
finally reach Mustang. Chogye Rinpoche's family maintains important
ties with Mustang, which lies in the border region between Tibet and
Nepal and is politically part of Nepal. Rinpoche's older sister was married to the previous king of Mustang, Jamphel Tenzin Dadul, who
offered support and protection when Rinpoche and his party escaped
Tibet. The present Mustang king, Jigme Palbar, is Chogye Rinpoche's
nephew, and the present Mustang queen is also a niece of Rinpoche.

After leaving Tibet, Chogye Trichen Rinpoche remained for some
time in Mustang, giving teachings and performing ritual prayers. The
majority of the monasteries in Mustang are of the Ngor branch of the
Sakya school, and the main monastery there was founded in the fifteenth century by Ngorchen Kunga Zangpo. Chogye Rinpoche has
often said that the architectural design of the palace of the Mustang
kings was created by Ngorchen Kunga Zangpo. Ngorchen spent time
in Mustang in the fifteenth century and was tremendously influential,
so most of the monasteries in Mustang belong to the Ngor branch of
the Sakya school. For over forty years, Chogye Trichen Rinpoche has
worked tirelessly to restore and revive the practice of Buddhism in
Mustang. He has firmly established in present-day Mustang the tradi-

tion of the Vinaya monastic vows, as well as the study and practice lineages of Mahayana and Vajrayana Buddhism.

For seven years, beginning from 1962, Chogye Rinpoche accepted the request of H. H. the Dalai Lama to serve as secretary general of the Council for Religious and Cultural Affairs of the Tibetan government-in-exile in Dharamsala, India. In this capacity he attended the World Sangha Conference held in Sri Lanka in 1965. Rinpoche took a leading role in preparing the manuscript of H. H. the Dalai Lama's book *My Land and My People* and wrote textbooks for schools set up for central Tibetans. It was in Dharamsala in November 1968 that Chogye Rinpoche met the great Christian contemplative Thomas Merton, as documented in Merton's *Asian Journal,* which includes a poem written by Rinpoche for the author.

In 1963 Chogye Rinpoche went on pilgrimage, visiting the Buddha's birthplace at Lumbini in southwestern Nepal. From early childhood, Rinpoche felt great devotion toward the place of Buddha's birth, and together with the Mustang king he resolved to build a monastery there. In 1967, Rinpoche and the king of Mustang appealed to His Majesty King Mahendra of Nepal, and in 1968 they were granted ten *katha* measures of land, under the supervision of the Department of Archaeology of the government of Nepal.

In 1969 Chogye Rinpoche took leave of the Tibetan government and returned to Nepal to re-create Nalendra Monastery and the seat of the Tsharpa school in exile. Rinpoche founded two monasteries in Nepal: the Tashi Rabten Ling Monastery in Lumbini, Nepal, and the Jamchen Lhakang Monastery beside the Bouddhanath stupa in Kathmandu, Nepal. The Tashi Rabten Ling Monastery in Lumbini was completed and dedicated in 1975. Chogye Rinpoche designed the Lumbini temple building and supervised the construction himself. He sold many precious things he had brought from Tibet to finance the monastery, which was additionally supported by the Mustang king and by the lay community. Chogye Rinpoche's younger sister, Jetsun Kusho Kunzang Tendrol, is a fully ordained nun and resides in the Lumbini monastery, where she has practiced meditation and offered prayers day and night for more than twenty-five years.

In addition to the Lumbini and Bouddhanath monasteries, a smaller retreat facility has been established by Rinpoche at Bagdora, near Shivapuri in the hills above Kathmandu. Bagdora is a sacred site blessed by Buddha Krakucchandra and other previous buddhas of our present "fortunate eon."

Chogye Rinpoche has also founded a Tsharpa retreat center at Lo Gekar in Mustang, a place where Guru Padmasambhava concealed treasure teachings and established a monastery prior to his founding the Samye Monastery in Tibet. Lo Gekar is a very sacred place; it was there that the *terton* Sangye Lama discovered the first "hidden treasure" (*terma*) teachings of Guru Padmasambhava. Sangye Lama was the first of the 108 *terton*s, revealers of treasure teachings, of the Nyingma tradition. There are many stories about Lo Gekar in the biographies of Guru Padmasambhava, such as the *Padma Kathang*.

In accord with the viewpoint of the Mahayoga tantras, the tantric histories tell us that the initial attempts to establish Samye Monastery in Tibet failed due to the power of the hostile ogress (*srin mo*) who controlled the land of Tibet. When Guru Padmasambhava located the head of the goddess at Lo Gekar, he concealed *terma* and established a monastery there. This was his first step toward taming the antagonistic forces and counteracting the inauspicious geomancy of the land of Tibet. Lo Gekar Monastery was offered to Chogye Rinpoche by the king of Mustang, and Rinpoche has spent a great deal of time in retreat there.

In keeping with the traditions of the Tsharpa lineage and Nalendra Monastery, Chogye Rinpoche has trained three groups of monks in the three-and-a-half-year meditation retreat of the tantric deity Hevajra. The first of these took place in Lumbini, Nepal, and was sponsored by H. H. the Dalai Lama; the second and third retreats took place at Bouddhanath in Kathmandu, Nepal. Through these retreats, Rinpoche has trained qualified retreat masters from all branches of the Sakya tradition who are capable of maintaining these practice lineages by supervising others in the practice of retreat. Chogye Rinpoche has requested that the Sakya and Ngor branches of the Sakya school now continue this tradition of the three-year retreat initiated by him.

As mentioned, since childhood Chogye Trichen Rinpoche has had strong faith toward Lumbini, the birthplace of the Buddha. Rinpoche has said that he first heard the life story of Buddha at the age of four or five, and when the name of Lumbini was mentioned, he was filled with such devotion that tears came to his eyes and a chill went through him such that the hairs of his body stood on end. The monastery at Lumbini has hosted H. H. the Dalai Lama, H. H. the Sixteenth Karmapa, H. H. Dilgo Khyentse Rinpoche, H. H. Sakya Trizin, Khunu Lama, and many other important lamas of all schools of Tibetan Buddhism.

At present Chogye Rinpoche is completing a second, much larger monastery in Lumbini, which will be the official seat and chief monastery of the Tsharpa branch of the Sakya school outside of Tibet. Every year, just before Tibetan New Year (*Losar*), Rinpoche and his monks conduct a ten- to fifteen-day ceremony of the tantric deities Mahakala and Mahakali. Rinpoche has also given there the entire Collection of Sadhanas (*Drubthab Kuntu*), a vast set of teachings requiring three months to transmit.

In addition to this, each year Chogye Rinpoche has upheld and supported the continuation of the annual Sakya Great Prayer (*Monlam*) festival for world peace in Lumbini. The Monlam festival is attended by H. H. Sakya Trizin and his two sons, as well as many other high lamas and *tulkus* of the Sakya school. The festival lasts for ten days and each year attracts over 3,000 monastic participants, in addition to thousands of lay devotees. The new monastery in Lumbini is being constructed to house the assembly that gathers for the annual Monlam prayer festival, which is held right at the birth site of Shakyamuni Buddha.

Chogye Rinpoche was requested by the king and queen of Nepal to improve conditions at the Buddha's birthplace in Lumbini. Visitors to Lumbini used to remark that in the stories of the Buddha's life, it was a splendid garden, one that was subsequently counted among the most famous in history, yet no flowers could be found there in the present time. In response to this situation and out of his devotion for the holy place, Chogye Rinpoche has established a large nursery at the new Lumbini monastery. The nursery now supplies several other nurseries and many gardens there, as part of Rinpoche's ongoing project to plant and maintain many gardens full of flowering trees and shrubs around Lumbini. These are well on their way to offering millions of flowers annually, honoring the birthplace of Buddha Shakyamuni.

King Birendra, the recently deceased king of Nepal, bestowed an asupicious title on Chogye Trichen Rinpoche. The name, Gorkha Dakshin Bau, means "Master of Western Nepal." It is the only time a Tibetan lama has been honored in this way by the king of Nepal. This honor was conferred by King Birendra in recognition of Rinpoche's Dharma activities, particularly his tireless work for the revival and renovation of Lumbini in western Nepal. These efforts include a book composed by Rinpoche, *Fortunate to Behold*, containing scriptural accounts of Lumbini found in the Tibetan Kangyur collection of the Buddhist canon. *Fortunate to Behold* has now been translated into English, Chinese, and Nepali.

As so many Tibetan Buddhist lineage holders have received teachings from Chogye Trichen Rinpoche, he is regarded as a supreme and holy master. Among his disciples are H. H. the Dalai Lama, to whom Rinpoche has offered many rare and precious instructions such as the *Lamdre Lobshe*; and H. H. Sakya Trizin, the head of the Sakya school. Rinpoche has transmitted his lineages to all the masters of the Sakya school, as well as to lamas of the Nyingma, Kagyu, and Gelug traditions, names too numerous to list in their entirety.

Chogye Trichen Rinpoche has been a teacher of H. H. the Dalai Lama since 1971. Rinpoche has the greatest devotion and respect for His Holiness as a refuge for sentient beings. His Holiness has said that he regards Chogye Rinpoche as one of his root gurus. Chogye Rinpoche has praised His Holiness for his understanding of the Lamdre, saying that this comes especially from his lifetime as the Fifth Dalai Lama, a great master of Lamdre. There are texts written by the Fifth Dalai Lama in the thirty-two-volume Lamdre canon. The Fifth Dalai Lama's main guru from the Sakya tradition was Gonpo Sonam Chogden, a master of the Tsharpa school who transmitted the uncommon Hevajra teachings, the Lamdre Lobshe, to the Fifth Dalai Lama. His Holiness the Fourteenth Dalai Lama received the Lamdre Lobshe from Chogye Trichen Rinpoche with great faith and confidence.

One interesting factor that explains the excellent synchronicity between Chogye Trichen Rinpoche and the Dalai Lama is the story of why His Holiness is known as the incarnation of the bodhisattva Avalokiteshvara. According to Chogye Rinpoche, the main reason the Dalai Lamas are known as incarnations of Avalokiteshvara is found in the story of the disciple of the Indian master Atisha, who was a Tibetan known as Dromtonpa Gyalwai Jungney. Atisha was a great Indian Buddhist pandita who founded the Kadam school of Buddhism and taught extensively in Tibet. His chief Tibetan disciple was Dromtonpa.

Dromtonpa was a true emanation of the bodhisattva Avalokiteshvara, or Chenrezig. In his famous work on the Kadam tradition, he confirms that first he was the bodhisattva Manjushri, then he was Buddha's disciple Shariputra, and then he was Dromtonpa. In the same work, he also confirms that he is the emanation of Avalokiteshvara. Also in the same work, it is mentioned that first there is Dromtonpa, then there is Gendun Drub, and similarly, that first there is Dromtonpa, then there is Khyenrab Choje. The reader will remember that Khyenrab Choje was the first in the succession of Chogye Trichens to come from the Zhalu Kushang family.

References and predictions from works of great teachers are relied upon to shed light on the origins of Dharma masters and their lineages. From these statements in the Kadam histories, it is understood that the First Dalai Lama, Gendun Drub, was known as the reincarnation of Dromtonpa and that this is the main reason the Dalai Lamas are known as emanations of Avalokiteshvara and Manjushri. The same text tells us that Khyenrab Choje was also the emanation of Dromtonpa, so he, too, is considered to be an emanation of Avalokiteshvara and Manjushri.

As mentioned above, from the time Khyenrab Choje held the title of Chogye Trichen, the Chogye Trichens have always been his descendants through the "bone lineage" of patrilineal heritage; hence, they are known as "bone lineage" *tulkus* or emanations. The Dalai Lamas have traditionally advised Nalendra Monastery to maintain their precious bone lineage in the selection of throne holders. It is said that the spiritual qualities of the previous masters can be transmitted to later masters through the bone lineage. This is why the stories of Khyenrab Choje and the subsequent Chogye Trichens are relevant to understanding the present Chogye Trichen.

It is thus understood that Dromtonpa has two lines of emanation that began with Gendun Drub and Khyenrab Choje, who were contemporaries: One line produced the Dalai Lamas through a lineage of reincarnations, and the other line produced the Chogye Trichens through the bone lineage of patrilineal descent. His Holiness the Dalai

Lama is the fourteenth such incarnation in his line, and the present Chogye Trichen is the eighteenth in his line of succession since Khyenrab Choje.

When asked about being the emanation of various bodhisattvas and masters, Chogye Trichen likes to joke that he does not really know about all that but feels certain that he is the reincarnation of his grandmother. When he was young, Rinpoche once dreamed that he broke his jaw. When he mentioned the dream to a relative, the relative remarked that Rinpoche's grandmother had broken her jaw in the same way. Rinpoche says that due to this, he must be her reincarnation!

Chogye Rinpoche has offered most of the major traditions he holds to H. H. Sakya Trizin, including: the uncommon Lamdre from the Tsharpa tradition; the Collection of Tantras (*Gyude Kuntu*), a compendium of teachings from all the major practice lineages of Tibetan Buddhism; the similar Collection of Sadhanas (*Drubthab Kuntu*); the Collected Works of Ngorchen Kunga Zangpo; the Hundred Teachings of the Jonang Tradition; six different Kalachakra initiations, four of which — the Bulug, Jonang, Maitri Gyatsha, and Domjung — are contained within the Gyude Kuntu; and many others. H. H. Sakya Trizin is the principal lineage holder of Chogye Trichen Rinpoche's Dharma lineages.

The Collection of Tantras is a vast repository of all the great practice traditions of Buddhism. It contains teachings and lineages of all Tibetan Buddhist schools and practice lineages, including the Nyingma, Sakya, Kagyu, Gelug, Bodong, Jonang, Zhije, Urgyen Nyengyu, and Kalachakra. There are 315 great initiations and 25 great commentaries, and it generally requires nearly two years to transmit in its entirety. Chogye Trichen Rinpoche was the only holder of the Collection of Tantras until he passed it to H. H. Sakya Trizin. This took place during several lengthy visits to the Sakya center in Dehra Dun, India, in the early 1970s. This lineage came to Chogye Rinpoche from Jamyang Loter Wangpo through Dampa Rinpoche, Zhenpen Nyingpo.

The great Sakya disciple of the incomparable Jamyang Khyentse Wangpo whose name was Jamyang Loter Wangpo compiled the Gyude Kuntu and Drubthab Kuntu under the instructions of his guru. When Jamyang Loter Wangpo transmitted these teachings in Kham, Dampa Rinpoche, Zhenpen Nyingpo, and the yogini Jetsun Pema were among his disciples. The famed yogini Jetsun Pema passed on this lineage of Drubthab Kuntu at Nalendra Monastery, with the previous Chogye Trichen and Zimog Rinpoche, guru of the present Chogye Trichen, as the main recipients. This is the tradition of Drubthab Kuntu that Chogye Rinpoche received from this teacher Zimog Rinpoche.

Jetsun Pema was a realized *siddha* yogini, having attained accomplishment in the practices of Hevajra and Vajrayogini. She was known to display many miraculous signs of accomplishment. When Jetsun Pema was teaching at Nalendra Monastery, she used to carry with her a coral mala. One day when answering the call of nature, she hung her mala on sunbeams, and many people witnessed it suspended there in the space.

On another occasion, Jetsun Pema visited northern Tibet to give a long life initiation. Some nuns were present, and they chided her, asking "Who are you, a woman, to give us initiation?" In response she removed her earrings and "hung" them in space, on the sunbeams coming in through a hole in the roof of the tent. Jetsun Pema was one of the real *dakinis*, female practitioners of great realization who displayed the genuine signs of accomplishment. This is one of the main reasons Chogye Rinpoche regards his particular lineage of Drubthab Kuntu as extremely precious.

In recent years, Rinpoche has given extensive teachings around the world. In 1988 he traveled to the United States and Canada, giving transmissions that included the initiation and complete instructions in the practice of the six-branch Vajrayoga of Kalachakra according to the Jonang tradition. Rinpoche has given the Kalachakra initiation in Tibet, Mustang, Kathmandu, Malaysia, the United States, Taiwan, and Spain, and is regarded by many as a definitive authority on Kalachakra.

Chogye Rinpoche has completed extensive retreat in the practice of Kalachakra, particularly of the six-branch yoga (*sadangayoga*) in the tradition of the Jonang school according to Jetsun Jonang Taranatha. In this way, Chogye Rinpoche has carried on the tradition of his predecessor, Khyenrab Choje, the incarnation of the Shambhala kings, who received the Kalachakra initiation from Vajrayogini herself. When Chogye Rinpoche was young, one of his teachers dreamed that Rinpoche was the son of the king of Shambhala, the pure land that upholds the tradition of Kalachakra.

In 1994 Rinpoche taught in Japan, granting such initiations as the great initiations of Buddha Maha Vairochana, whose practice has historically been widespread in Japan. In 1996, he made his first teaching visit to Australia. In 1998, Rinpoche made one of several tours to Singapore, Malaysia, Hong Kong, Taiwan, and Australia, giving many initiations and teachings. In the same year, Rinpoche bestowed the Kalachakra initiation and other teachings in Taipei, Taiwan, to an assembly of 6,000 disciples that included the mayor of Taipei and several ministers of the government of Taiwan.

In 2000, Chogye Rinpoche visited France, where he bestowed initiations from the Collection of Sadhanas (*Drubthab Kuntu*). In the same year, Rinpoche gave the Kalachakra initiation and public teachings in Barcelona, Spain. Most recently, in 2001, Rinpoche completed a two-month teaching tour to Hong Kong and Taiwan, to five cities in Australia, and to New Zealand, Singapore, and Kuching in Malaysia.

Outside of Tibet and Nepal, Chogye Rinpoche has centers in Hong Kong and Taiwan, as well as a large property currently under construction as a retreat center at Vista Bella in Spain. Rinpoche is also the spiritual patron of centers in Australia and New Zealand. He gave teachings including the initiations of Hevajra and Chakrasamvara, as well as the uncommon instructions on the practice of Vajrayogini, at the Australian centers during the 1996 and 2001 visits.

Those who have received an audience or teachings from Chogye Rinpoche will no doubt agree that he is an avid storyteller. Almost every teaching or initiation given by Rinpoche is accompanied by wonderful stories about the particular bodhisattvas or teachers of that lineage, as well as stories that illustrate the main teachings of the Buddha, such as renunciation, compassion, bodhichitta, and devotion.

Chogye Rinpoche exchanged many teachings with H. H. Dilgo Khyentse Rinpoche, former head of the Nyingma school. Dilgo Khyentse Rinpoche said that he regarded Chogye Trichen as the emanation (*tulku*) of Chetsun Senge Wangchuk, the renowned *dzogchen* master of eleventh- to twelfth-century Tibet who attained the great transformation rainbow body (*jalus phowa chenpo*). An example of the auspicious connections between Chogye Rinpoche and Dilgo Khyentse Rinpoche is that Khyentse Rinpoche was known as the incarnation of Vimalamitra, the Indian master who was one of the founders of

Tibetan Buddhism. Several hundred years after his departure from Tibet, Vimalamitra reappeared in the rainbow light body and imparted his teachings to Chetsun Senge Wangchuk. In addition, Chogye Rinpoche regarded Dilgo Khyentse Rinpoche as the incarnation of Rabsel, a future buddha of our fortunate eon. This is significant in view of the relation of the Chogye Trichens with the future buddha Maitreya.

The sublime master Tulku Urgyen Rinpoche has stated that Chogye Trichen Rinpoche is a *siddha*, an accomplished practitioner of the Vajrayana Buddhist path. In this regard, we can mention a few examples that may be seen to illustrate this. In Vajrayana Buddhism, the teachings speak of the three roots: the guru, or lama; the meditation deity, or *yidam*; and the *dakini*s and Dharma protectors.

Concerning the first, the accomplishment of the guru or lama, there is a story recounted by Chogye Rinpoche's attendant Wangdu-la. Chogye Rinpoche was staying in Lumbini in the 1970s, residing in his room upstairs in the monastery. Wangdu-la was resting in the next room when he heard Chogye Rinpoche speaking in a full voice as though he were giving teachings. In the morning Rinpoche asked him, "Did you hear anything last night? Last night, I was very fortunate. I had a pure vision of Ngorchen Kunga Zangpo." Rinpoche confided that Ngorchen appeared above and in front of him and reached down his hand to him. Rinpoche indicated that he took hold of Ngorchen's hand and held it to the crown of his head with deep devotion.

Continuing to hold Ngorchen's hand, Chogye Rinpoche gave a complete commentary on the famous praise to Ngorchen Kunga Zangpo known as *Rab kar ma*, as an offering to Ngorchen. Rinpoche commented to Wangdu-la that Ngorchen was a great master, who had carefully observed the monastic vows of the Vinaya, just as Rinpoche himself did; and further, that they both held and practiced the lineage of Hevajra and the Lamdre Lobshe. For these reasons, Ngorchen was pleased with Chogye Rinpoche and granted him the pure vision of his wisdom body.

Along these lines, as signs of the *yidam* meditation deity, a few stories may be mentioned. During his early life in Tibet, Chogye Rinpoche gave a great many Vajrayana initiations and teachings and performed meditation retreats every year. To signify his accomplishments, many auspicious signs have accompanied his Dharma activities. One of Chogye Rinpoche's close disciples reported that once when Rinpoche bestowed the thirteen-day initiation of Maha Vairochana, on the concluding day he gave an initiation of White Mahakala. On that occasion, a hundred butter lamps were lit on the shrine as offerings. At one point, the flames from all the lamps were seen to join together into a single large flame, which rose up higher and higher, rotating clockwise, and then disappeared into the sky. This was witnessed by all those present.

Another story that recounts how the signs of the meditation deity were displayed relates to the time when Chogye Rinpoche gave the Lamdre in Mustang in 1977 at the Tsarang Monastery, which was established by Ngorchen Kunga Zangpo (1382–1456). The throne in Tsarang Monastery is the throne of Ngorchen. During the 1977 visit to Mustang, Rinpoche gave the Lamdre for a period of one and a half months and also conducted the traditional three-month monsoon retreat for monks there.

To reach Mustang, one must travel from Pokhara to Jomsom in northern Nepal by horse. There are several rivers that must be crossed on horseback during the journey. When Chogye Rinpoche was crossing a broad river there, a very large rainbow appeared continuously around Rinpoche and his horse, all the way across the river. There were fifteen or twenty people all around Rinpoche, and some thought that the rainbow might have been caused by the sun's reflection on the spray thrown up by Rinpoche's horse. Yet there was no rainbow surrounding any of the other riders, and the rainbow seemed spherical in shape and followed Rinpoche all the way across the river, as witnessed by everyone in the party.

When they reached Tsarang Monastery and Chogye Rinpoche began giving the Lamdre, he announced that he would not eat after twelve o'clock noon and would not meet anyone outside of the teachings but should be left alone during those times. As the Lamdre progressed into the section on the "three tantras" or "three continuums" (*gyu sum*), Rinpoche seemed to give no thought to time and would often remain on the throne until midnight, without breaking for tea or meals. The following morning Rinpoche would always appear on time and seem quite normal but again remain on the throne without breaking for meals or tea, as the day before. Sometimes, after midnight, Rinpoche would have to be carried off the throne, all the while continuing his teaching as if nothing had happened, immersed in the pure vision of the mandala of Hevajra. This continued for fifteen days. During this time, Rinpoche's face often seemed transfigured, and his gaze at times reminded those present of the faces of tantric deities such as Hevajra.

As the summer monastic retreat was being conducted during the same period, each evening during those months, at five or six o'clock, the monks would recite prayers and circumambulate the monastery. During the time when the Lamdre was being given, a rainbow appeared almost every evening at the time the monks would make their rounds. Often the rainbow would appear to descend from the sky and touch down on the monastery. Also during these days, a circular rainbow would be seen around the sun. At the end of the summer retreat, the monks celebrate with a picnic, and they went to a garden meadow near Tsarang Monastery. On that day, a rainbow could be seen stretching from the monastery all the way to the garden park.

Some disciples feared that all of this might portend that the lama would soon pass away, and many ceremonies dedicated to the long life of Rinpoche were offered by the Mustang royal family and others. When the Lamdre had been given and the summer retreat concluded, Chogye Rinpoche mentioned to his attendant, who was named Guru, that people seemed to think that all of these rainbow signs meant he was going to pass away but that this was not the case. Rinpoche confided that these rainbows were, instead, an auspicious indication that Ngorchen Kunga Zangpo was happy with him for following and maintaining his teachings, for sitting on his throne, and for carrying out his wishes. The rainbow signs were indications of Ngorchen's blessings, due to his being pleased with Chogye Rinpoche's extensive Dharma activities in Mustang. From this story we can see evidence of the blessings of the meditation deity Hevajra and of the blessings of the lama, Ngorchen Kunga Zangpo.

Another incident in Chogye Rinpoche's life that might also be mentioned in regard to the meditation deity (*yidam*), concerns Rinpoche's trip to Kuching, Malaysia, in 1989. Rinpoche was invited to give the great initiation of Kalachakra according to the Jonang tradition, as well as the complete instructions on the six-branch yoga (*sadangayoga*) of the Kalachakra of the Jonangpas, according to the practice manual of Jonang Taranatha.

It is customary that in preparation for an initiation, the *chopon*, or ritual attendant, must set out and array the physical representation of the mandala for consecration in the ritual. Generally, Chogye Rinpoche would allow the *chopon* to simply follow the textual instructions and prepare the mandala as he had been taught, without adding many instructions. However, on this occasion, Rinpoche instructed the *chopon*, his attendant named Guru, to make the mandala very properly. Rinpoche sat with him and guided him in detail how to prepare it. A metal plate was brought and coated with a thin layer of butter to make it slightly sticky, and on it were arrayed pieces of corn to represent all the deities of the mandala. Then, as Rinpoche was doing his preparations for the initiation, his appearance became quite powerful.

During the initiation of Kalachakra, at the time of the consecration of the physical representation of the mandala by the deities of the wisdom mandala, Rinpoche explained that the deities of the mandala of Kalachakra were now actually present above the physical mandala on the shrine. One of those present remarked that when Rinpoche said this, his words had unusual weight, as though he were clearly seeing this for himself.

Following the initiation, as the *chopon* was clearing the shrine, he noticed clear markings on the mandala plate. The markings were not below the film of butter nor were they on top of it, but they appeared within the film of butter. There were eight clear flower shapes at eight points around the edge of the plate, and two in the center of the plate, making a total of ten flower patterns or "lotuses." This was seen by everyone and was photographed.

In the mandala of Kalachakra, there are the two central deities of Buddha Kalachakra and his consort, Vishvamata, surrounded by the eight dakinis, or *shakti*s as they are called in Kalachakra, just as one finds in the mandalas of other tantric buddhas such as Hevajra or Chakrasamvara. Thus, the flower markings are understood as signs of the actual presence of the deities. In the biographies of the lineage masters, one of the signs of accomplishment is "flowers" in the mandala. These are described in the texts in two ways, either as naturally appearing on or within the mandala, as was the case in this instance, or else as descending or falling onto the mandala.

Chogye Trichen Rinpoche is respected as one of the true masters of ritual prayer and initiation. In this regard, one final story demonstrating the blessings of the tantric deities (*yidam*) is worth repeating. Chogye Rinpoche has frequently been requested by His Holiness the Dalai Lama and the Tibetan government-in-exile to perform various rituals. Once, when Rinpoche performed the fire puja of the female tantric deity Kurukulla, the Dalai Lama remarked, "The teachings and rituals of the Sakyapas are very profound and always bring good results."

Shortly thereafter, the Dalai Lama left the room where the prayers were taking place, and just then a mild earthquake occurred. Returning immediately, the Dalai Lama commented, "You see, I told you the Sakya teachings are very profound. Here is a sign to prove it!" The earth shook five more times during the course of that ritual, and some of those present noted that auspicious events in the life of the Buddha had been accompanied by earth tremors. Since that time, there has been a special shrine to Kurukulla in the Dalai Lama's palace in honor of that auspicious consecration.

Having mentioned signs of the blessings of the guru (*lama*) and of the meditation deities (*yidam*), there are also incidents that demonstrate the blessings of the female deities (*dakinis*) and Dharma protectors. In 1959, after the Lhasa uprising in the face of the Chinese invasion of Tibet, Chogye Rinpoche dreamed of a man riding a black horse, enormous in size. The man said to him, "I will give you the passport to leave here." Then a woman, white in color and dressed as a Buddhist nun, appeared to him in the dream, and said, "Here is your passport." With this, she handed him a document. Rinpoche has confided that these two are Dugyal and Karmo, two protectors associated with the deity Vajrakilaya and with Guru Padmasambhava. These are the same protectors associated with the life of Sachen Kunga Nyingpo who appeared at Sakya to warn that Sachen had fallen ill at the seminary where he was studying. It was due to these events that Chogye Rinpoche built a shrine to Dugyal once he had safely reached Mustang.

Chogye Rinpoche made the decision to leave Tibet two days after the Chinese occupied Lhasa. Rinpoche consulted a holy female protector deity, and she instructed him to leave but to go to the north; Rinpoche had earlier thought to escape together with His Holiness the Dalai Lama to the south. Rinpoche followed the guidance of his protector and was successful, in spite of Chinese planes flying overhead and bombs exploding around them. Chogye Rinpoche made his way to the safe haven of Lo Monthang in Mustang, just within Nepal on the Tibetan border.

There is one last story that might be mentioned here in relation to the Dharma protectors, an unusual event that took place during one of Rinpoche's trips to Mustang. Chogye Rinpoche went to Mustang a great many times, and every village would invite him to perform ceremonial prayers and give teachings. There was just one particular village in northeastern Mustang, called Samdzong, that for many years had never invited Rinpoche to visit. This village depended on a spring some way up the valley to supply a river that watered their crops. One year, this spring dried up, and the river did not begin until some way down the valley, below the fields of that village. The villagers feared they would have no crops, and invited Rinpoche to come to their aid.

Chogye Rinpoche went to the village and performed three days of prayer ceremonies; he also made some divinations. Then Rinpoche said, "Now I must go to where the source of the stream used to be." Everyone in Rinpoche's party, including the king of Mustang, traveled the four kilometers upstream on horseback. Carpets were placed on the ground next to where the spring had been, together with a small throne; a stone was placed as a table for Rinpoche.

Then Rinpoche began his prayers, making the *torma* offering and incense offering to the *naga*s. Shortly after beginning these prayers, the carpets and throne had to be quickly moved, as the spring suddenly began to overflow, gushing water and flooding the area where they had been sitting. Everyone had to move quite far back from the spring due to the force of the water. From that time to the present day, the spring has flowed abundantly, and the farmers of that village have never wanted for water for their crops. This incident brings to mind stories found in the biographies of the great masters that speak of their bringing forth water in places where there was none.

Chogye Rinpoche is very famous among the Dharma community in Nepal for his "mantra water." Over the years, people have regularly brought bottles of mineral water, into which Rinpoche has placed sacred blessing medicine. Then Rinpoche has blown mantras over and into the tops of the bottles. Even a small amount of this water is highly prized by those who know of its effects, and a great many people have avoided operations and serious diseases after faithfully ingesting it. This is widely known around Bouddhanath, in Nepal where Rinpoche resides.

Many Tibetan Buddhist lamas confirm what stories such as these suggest. Karma Thinley Rinpoche mentions that Chogye Rinpoche has realized the vajra body, the fruit of tantric accomplishment. Tsikey Chokling Rinpoche has confided that Chogye Rinpoche has completely exhausted all *kleshas*, or afflictive emotions, all karma, and all concepts into the nature of reality (*dharmata*); and that Rinpoche is one of those most rare living Buddhist masters who dwell always in that realized state.

Since his early youth, Chogye Rinpoche has remained in meditation daily in four sessions of four to five hours each, a discipline he has upheld down to the present day. At times, Rinpoche may complete the full sadhanas of Hevajra or other deities two or three times in a session. Rinpoche is assisted by the fact that he has for his whole life slept only an hour or an hour and a half per night.

It is this ability to practice constantly without the need for sleep that has allowed Rinpoche to maintain the daily recitation commitments for many precious Sakya practice lineages, unbroken lineages of daily recitation that might otherwise have been interrupted at the time the lamas fled the Chinese invasion of Tibet. It is due to his devotion to spiritual practice that Chogye Rinpoche has come to be regarded by many as a uniquely accomplished meditation master, the heart of the practice lineage of the Sakya school.

Chogye Rinpoche spent the better part of the decade, from when he turned seventy until he was eighty, accumulating the retreat commitments of the deity Mahakala. Rinpoche's retreat practice of this tradition of Mahakala actually began in 1978 with a six-month retreat at the royal palace in Mustang. It is thought that by now Rinpoche has performed the equivalent of at least two three-year retreats on the tantric deity Mahakala.

It is often said that Chogye Rinpoche maintains the style of a hidden yogi. It is because Rinpoche spends so much time in meditation retreat that he is regarded as a hidden master. He has completed the equivalent of several three-year meditation retreats. To this day he remains about twenty hours a day in meditation and prayer, following the example of past Buddhist *siddha*s such as Virupa in India and Milarepa in Tibet. In 2002, Rinpoche turned eighty-three, maintaining still this extraordinary level of practice and Dharma activity.

His Holiness Sakya Trizin has spoken of Chogye Trichen Rinpoche thus: "There are many who have attained the wisdom arising from the study of the scriptures. There are some who have attained the wisdom arising from the contemplation of the Dharma. There are few who have gained wisdom arising from meditation. Chogye Trichen Rinpoche is one who has attained all three wisdoms. One should consider oneself fortunate just to meet him, which is in itself a great blessing."

Part One:
The Root Text

*The Pith Instruction on the Mind Training
Teaching of Parting from the Four Attachments*

by Jetsun Drakpa Gyaltsen

The Pith Instruction on the Mind Training Teaching of Parting from the Four Attachments

by Jetsun Drakpa Gyaltsen

May the kind teachers and compassionate tantric deities
In whom I take refuge from my heart
Please bestow blessings upon me.

It is unnecessary to act without [regard for] Dharma.
As for the manner of accomplishing Dharma,
I request you to listen to this instruction on
Parting from the Four Attachments.

*Thus, the invocation and promise to explain the teaching
have been made by the author.*[*]

> If you are attached to this life,
> you are not a person of Dharma.
> If you are attached to cyclic existence,
> you do not have renunciation.
> If you are attached to your own purpose,
> you do not have bodhichitta.
> If grasping arises,
> you do not have the view.

First, for non-attachment to this life,
You must put aside the non-Dharma person's [manner of]
Practicing moral conduct, hearing, contemplation, and meditation,

---

[*] The annotations indicated in italics are by Sakya Pandita.

Which are performed for the sake of this life.

To begin with, moral conduct is explained as endowing [one] with
The root for accomplishing the higher realms,
The ladder for attaining liberation,
And the antidote by which one abandons suffering.

Though there is no method [for gaining liberation]
Without moral conduct,
The moral conduct of one attached to this life is endowed with
The root for accomplishing the eight worldly concerns,
Denigration of [those possessing] inferior moral conduct,
Jealousy toward the righteous,
Hypocrisy in one's own moral conduct,
And the seed for attaining the lower realms.
Put aside this false moral conduct.

The person who undertakes hearing and contemplation
Is endowed with the wealth for accomplishing knowledge,
The lamp that dispels ignorance,
The knowledge of the path by which to guide living beings,
And the seed of the *dharmakaya*.

Though there is no method [for gaining liberation]
Without hearing and contemplation,
One who hears and contemplates while attached to this life
Is endowed with the wealth that accomplishes pride,
Contempt for [those] inferior in hearing and contemplation,
Jealousy toward those who possess hearing and contemplation,
The pursuit of followers and wealth,
And the root [causes] for attaining the lower realms.
Put aside this hearing and contemplation [based on]
The eight worldly concerns.

All persons who practice meditation
Are endowed with the antidote
For abandoning the afflictive emotions,

The root for accomplishing the path to liberation,
And the seed for attaining buddhahood.

Though there is no method [for gaining liberation]
Without meditation,
The meditator who practices for the sake of this life
Is busy though living in seclusion:
Reciting prayers by blindly chanting words,
Ridiculing those who hear and contemplate,
Jealous of others who meditate,
And distracted in his own meditation;
Cast aside this meditation of the eight worldly concerns.

What has been written up to this point is in accordance with the
Abhidharmakosha, *where it states, "Through possessing hearing and*
contemplation based upon moral conduct, one should thoroughly apply
oneself to meditation." Thus, this shows directly the distinction between
ultimate and relative aims, whereas it indicates indirectly the manner
of meditating upon the difficulty of obtaining the [eighteen]
prerequisites [of human rebirth] and upon the impermanence of life.

In order to attain nirvana,
Abandon attachment to the three realms.
In order to abandon attachment to the three realms,
Keep in mind the faults of worldly existence.

First, the suffering of suffering
Is the suffering of the three lower realms.
If this is contemplated well, one's flesh will tremble.
If it befalls one, there is no way one could bear it.

Those who do not accomplish the virtue of abandoning it
Are cultivators of the lower realms.
Wherever they reside, they are pitiful.

When contemplating the suffering of change, one sees:
The movement [of beings] from heavenly realms

To the lower realms;
Shakra reborn as an ordinary being;
The sun and moon going dark;
And the universal emperor reborn as a slave.

Belief in this depends upon the word [of the Buddha],
As ordinary people do not have the ability to realize it,
So observe for yourself the changes of men:
The wealthy become poor, the mighty become weak,
Where there were many people there is [only] one, and so on,
Exceeding the imagination.

When contemplating the suffering
Of the nature of all conditional phenomena, one sees:
No end to activities,
That suffering exists among many and among few,
And that suffering exists among the rich and the poor.

All of human life is exhausted in preparations,
And everyone dies while making preparations.
Those preparations do not end even at the time of death,
[When we] begin preparations for the next life.

Those who are attached to this world of existence,
Which is a heap of suffering, are pitiful.

*Up to this point, the faults of the world of existence have been directly
shown, whereas what actions should be taken up and [what should be]
rejected have been indirectly indicated in accordance with the law of
cause and result.*

When free from attachment, nirvana is won.
When nirvana is attained, bliss is obtained.
This song of experience is the
Parting from the Four Attachments.

Liberating myself alone is without benefit,
Since all the sentient beings of the three realms are my parents.
To leave my parents in the midst of suffering
While desiring my own bliss is pitiful.

Let the sufferings of the three realms of existence ripen upon me,
And let my merits be taken by sentient beings.
By the blessings of this merit
May all sentient beings attain buddhahood.

*Up to this point, the meditations on loving kindness and compassion,
which are the causes [for the production of the enlightenment thought],
have been indirectly indicated, whereas exchanging self and others,
which is the result [of the enlightenment thought], has been shown
directly.*

In whatever manner I continue, there is no liberation
Through grasping at the true nature of things.
To explain this precisely:
There is no liberation through grasping at existence,
There are no heavenly realms through grasping at non-existence,
[And] grasping at both [extremes] is [only] done in ignorance.
Be joyful in the state of non-duality.

*Up to this point, having rejected the views of eternalism and nihilism,
the general method for placing the mind in the non-dual state [of the
inseparable merging of subject and object, existence and non-existence,
and so on] has been shown.*

All phenomena are mind's sphere of experience.
Do not seek a creator in the four elements,
In chance, in God, or the like,
But be joyful in the nature of mind itself.

*Up to this point, having shown the stages of the path common to the
Bodhisattva Vijñanavada (Mind Only) school, now the uncommon
path of the Mahayana Madhyamaka school will be explained.*

Appearances are of the nature of magical illusions,
Arising through interdependence.
Not knowing how to describe their natural state,
Be joyful in the ineffable.

*Up to this point, the manner of meditating upon calm abiding
meditation [shamatha] has been indirectly indicated, whereas the
manner of meditating on clear insight [vipasyana] has been directly
shown in the following way: Having systematically established that all
objective outer appearances are mind made; that [the mind] is illusory;
that [the illusion] is without an inherent nature of its own; and that
[the natureless illusion] is interdependent in origin and inexpressible,
one meditates on the merging [of the mind and its true nature of
emptiness], the Absolute devoid of all conceptual extremes.*

By the merit of this virtue
Of explaining the Parting From the Four Attachments,
May all the seven races of living beings
Be established upon the stage of buddhahood.

*The author concludes with the dedication of merit and indicates the
result.*

Colophon:
This instruction on Parting from the Four Attachments was written
by the yogi Drakpa Gyaltsen at the auspicious Sakya monastery.

Part Two:
The Commentary

Commentary On Parting from the
Four Attachments

by Chogye Trichen Rinpoche

1. History

✍

THE SUBJECT WE WILL DISCUSS is the famous teaching known as Parting from the Four Attachments (*Zhenpa Zhidrel*). This teaching is the very quintessence of all of the teachings of all of the buddhas of the three times. The entire pith instructions, the key oral instructions for practice, are presented here in the simplest possible form. This means that everyone can apply these instructions to their own lives and will find them practical and useful. In order to gain the greatest benefit from receiving these teachings, it is important to generate the appropriate state of mind. Resolve to turn your mind toward these Mahayana Buddhist teachings in order to benefit innumerable sentient beings.

Among the many types of Dharma, this teaching on Parting from the Four Attachments addresses the topic the training of the mind (*lojong*). The purpose of the mind training teachings is to make the mind flexible, or pliable — that is, to soften our habitual rigidity. The mind of an untrained person is likened to new leather. If it is left untreated, leather will become stiffer, more rigid and tough. Once the leather has been worked properly, then however you may wish to fold it or use it, it will accommodate your wishes. On the other hand, there is not much you can do with untreated leather.

Following this analogy, the intention of mind training is that we can train our minds to become more supple in order to soften our character. There is a famous prayer in which the disciple prays, "Please bless me that my mind may be trained by the Mahayana teachings." The spiritual teacher particularly appreciates those disciples who have trained their minds.

The teachings of the three vehicles of Buddhism, namely the Theravadan trainings of renunciation and refuge, the Mahayana trainings of love and compassion, and the Vajrayana trainings of deity yoga, mantra, and samadhi, are all applied to one's own mind in order to soften rigid patterns and make the mind more amenable. The intent of the three vehicles of training is to help us to eliminate the three mental poisons of attachment, aversion, and ignorance.

If the trainings are applied well, they will serve us well, since every practice we do will benefit us greatly, and we will become more relaxed and at ease as a result. Once the mind has been trained properly by the application of the teachings, there is not much more guidance one needs from the teacher in regard to mind training; already one is doing one's best. If the teachings truly lessen the presence of the three mental poisons of attachment, aversion, and ignorance in our own experience, this is the sign of successfully training the mind. If these afflictive emotions are not diminished, this means we are not practicing correctly.

Mind training has a great variety of sources and texts in all the different Buddhist traditions of Tibet. We can see that initially the Kadam masters of the eleventh century wrote many texts on the practice of mind training. This was followed by the early teachers of the Sakya tradition, as well as by the masters of the Kagyu school, the tradition of the early great meditators of Tibet. These include Gampopa, who authored the famous *Jewel Ornament of Liberation*. This in turn was followed by the teachings on the graduated path to enlightenment (*lamrim*) of Lama Tsongkhapa, founder of the Gelug school. For the followers of Sakya, the tradition of Parting from the Four Attachments is held in particular esteem among the teachings on mind training.

In order to approach the Sakya tradition in the proper context, one must know that there are five major schools in the Tibetan Buddhist tradition: the Nyingma, the Kadam, the Kagyu, the Gelug, and the Sakya. Each of these schools produced in turn five great founding masters. This teaching on Parting from the Four Attachments originated with the first of the five founding masters of the Sakya school, who was known as Sachen Kunga Nyingpo, of the ancient and blessed Khon family of Tibet.

Parting from the Four Attachments, like other mind training teachings from all Tibetan Buddhist traditions, is held to epitomize a wealth of important instructions received directly from a lineage of enlightened masters. In learning this teaching, it is helpful to know something of the upholders of the lineage, the family known in Tibet as the Khon family, the holders of the Sakya tradition. To begin with, I want to share with you some of the special qualities of the Sakya lineage, sometimes known as the lineage possessing three excellent names. These three excellent names illustrate how the hereditary lineage of the Sakyas has come about.

The first of these excellent names is "the hereditary lineage of the gods." To understand the reason for this name, we must know that the origin of the upholders of this lineage is found among the progenitors of the Tibetan people. There are many hereditary lineages that make up the Tibetan people. Among these, there are six that are held in the highest esteem; these are known as the six principal family lineages of Tibet. These six families are believed to have descended from the *devas*, or gods. Among these six, there are two families originating with these gods of clear light, or *prabhashvara-devas*, whose descendants have continued to benefit the human race. These two families are called Khon and Zhalu, and are known to have preserved the purity of their hereditary lineages.

In the beginning, it is said that from among these original founders of the Tibetan people, there were three gods dwelling in the realm of the gods of clear light, named Kering, Ngoring, and Tsering, who descended from their celestial abodes into this world. It is said that they entered our world at Shelkar, "Crystal Mountain," which is located in the mountain range known as Namla in the far northern part of Tibet, in the border region between Tibet and Mongolia. These gods who had come down with their entourages enjoyed great wealth and splendor. It is said that they displayed various signs of the wealth gods, such as the wish-fulfilling cow, and dwelt in the sky in a golden celestial mansion, a palace studded with turquoise and fine precious stones and jewels.

At the time of their descent, they came to reside near the summits of the mountains in the Namla range. In those ancient times, there were some demonic beings who dwelt in the foothills of those mountains and in caverns below their base. Sometime after their arrival in our world, the three gods and their descendants deemed it necessary to subdue some of these demonic forces that frequented Tibet in those times.

The gods found themselves in a long and protracted conflict between their own tribe and a group of non-human demonic beings of the class of *raksha*s, as they are known in India. Finally, the gods triumphed, and the king of the descended gods of clear light slew the king of the *raksha*s, whose name was Sinpo Drakmema. In this way, the *raksha* tribe was defeated.

One of the daughters of the *raksha* beings was an exquisitely beautiful princess called Yatuk Silima. During the course of the battle between the gods and the *raksha*s, a love affair developed between the *raksha* princess Yatuk Silima and one of the three principal gods who came down, the prince named Ngoring. They were joined in marriage, and out of their matrimony a child was born and given the name Khon Bar-kye. *Khon* means "resentment" or "hostility" in Tibetan; *bar* means "in between"; and *kye* means "born into." Thus, the full meaning of the name is "born in the midst of hostility." It is also understood to mean "one born between hostility and love," that is, one who is a mixture of these two qualities. This and similar events heralded the beginning of the Tibetan people.

From this story we learn that the source of the Khon family was in the realm of the gods of clear light (*osal*), the *prabhashvara-deva*s, who inhabit one of the seventeen god realms of the realm of form. It was from this heaven of the Clear Light Gods that the celestial ancestors of the Khon family descended to our world many thousands of years ago. Thus, the Khon family is known as the "descendants of the gods of clear light." It is due to the unique historical facts of their origin that the first of their excellent names is "the hereditary lineage of the gods." The family line produced as a result of this "love born of conflict" thus came to be known in Tibet as the Khon family. Hence, the second excellent name of the Sakya family is "the hereditary lineage of the Khon family."

The Khon family has produced an abundance of holy descendants with great spiritual blessings throughout the generations. From Khon Bar-kye onward, the descendants of the lineage flourished. For example, masters such as Khon Dorje Rinchen were holders of many of the earliest Nyingma lineages. Numerous great masters came from this family during the initial era of Tibetan Buddhism, which later came to be known as the Nyingma, or Old Translation, period.

The Old Translation period was initiated by Guru Padmasambhava, who brought the Dharma to Tibet during the first spreading of the

Buddha's teachings there. Guru Padmasambhava had twenty-five major disciples. Among them, Khon Lu Wangpo of the Khon family was one of the most prominent, as well as being one of the original seven Tibetans to be ordained as Buddhist monks. Khon Lu Wangpo was particularly adept in the practice of Vajrakilaya, so the tradition of Vajrakilaya esteemed and propagated by the Khon family originates with him. He attained accomplishment (*siddhi*) through the practice of Vajrakilaya at the place called Drak Yerpa, not far from Lhasa.

From the time of Khon Lu Wangpo right to the present day, all the holders of the hereditary practice lineage of the Khon family have been accomplished masters (*siddha*s) of the meditational deity Vajrakilaya and have demonstrated miraculous signs. The early masters of the Khon family mainly followed the teachings of the Nyingma school, such as the meditation deity Vajrakilaya and many others.

The Khon lineage continued on down to two brothers, who were the real founders of the Dharma tradition of the Khon family. These were Khon Konchog Gyalpo and his older brother, Khon Rog Sherab Tsultrim. Sherab Tsultrim was an accomplished master of Vajrakilaya who is said to have plunged his ritual dagger (*phurba*) into the rocky cliffs of the Nyak region north of Sakya. His younger brother, Khon Konchog Gyalpo, was the father of Sachen Kunga Nyingpo, who received the four lines of Parting from the Four Attachments directly from Manjushri.

Khon Konchog Gyalpo met many translators and scholars who had traveled to and from India, and he became quite interested in the teachings of the New Translation period that were being transmitted in Tibet in those times. Though his predecessors had done very well following the teachings of the Old Translation period, generally attaining accomplishment through the meditation deities Yandag Heruka and Vajrakilaya, he nonetheless began to develop great interest in the teachings of the Sarma, the New Translation teachings.

Having met the translator Drokmi Lotsawa, who had returned from extensive studies in India, Khon Konchog Gyalpo took him as his teacher and resolved to follow the New Translation teachings. Khon Konchog Gyalpo decided to build a monastery at a place called Sakya in central Tibet. The name comes from a rocky cliff found in that area that is part of a grayish landscape and hence was called Sakya, or "gray earth." The monastery and the tradition he established have come to be named after the landscape in that area.

Once the great monastery at Sakya was founded, the name of Sakya came to be more commonly associated with the family than their original name of Khon. The Sakya Monastery has been regarded as the seat of great *vajradharas* (vajra holders). It has even been said that the members of the glorious Sakya clan resemble the noble snow lion in appearance.

When Khon Konchok Gyalpo, the founder of the Sakya Monastery, had passed away, his son Sachen was still quite young, so one of the great masters and translators of those times, Bari Lotsawa, was chosen to be successor to the throne. Bari Lotsawa had traveled to India and lived there many years learning Sanskrit; hence, he was widely respected. The responsibility for the education and upbringing of Konchog Gyalpo's son, Sachen Kunga Nyingpo, fell to the boy's mother.

Sachen's mother was very intelligent, an innovative and highly capable woman, and she realized that her son required a special teacher. With this in mind, she appointed Bari Lotsawa as his personal tutor, which allowed Sachen to further his studies and practice while remaining at Sakya. Through her skillful guidance, Sachen's mother was able to exert a significant influence on the circumstances under which Sachen was to be raised. By her many activities on his behalf, she has been deemed worthy of the greatest respect for ably honoring her significant duties.

At this point in the life story of Sachen Kunga Nyingpo, we reach the episode in the history of the Khon family that shows how they gained the third excellent name by which they are known, "the miraculous hereditary lineage of Manjushri." Let us now recount the story of how the Khon family came to be blessed by Manjushri.

Having been invested with the worthy task of educating the young throne holder, Bari Lotsawa explained the situation to Sachen thus: "Since you are the lineage holder of Sakya, belonging to a very blessed family, you are not like an ordinary child going through a conventional religious education. You may have been born with intelligence as a result of your family heritage, but it is nevertheless important for you to study, contemplate, and meditate. In order to do this effectively, it is necessary to unfold extraordinary qualities of intelligence.

"You may also have inherited the benefits of intelligence developed in past lifetimes, which can be regained through deliberate study. Still, to properly succeed in your spiritual training, you must develop wisdom. In order to enhance and heighten your natural gifts, it is important to resort to the practice of a wisdom deity. For this reason, although there are many varieties of meditational deities, you should rely on a wisdom deity and enter the practice of the bodhisattva Manjushri. I suggest that you undertake a retreat of Orange Manjushri."

With this proclamation, Bari Lotsawa bestowed upon Sachen the empowerment of Orange Manjushri, known as the *Arapatsana* empowerment. He then asked Sachen, a youth of only twelve years, to go into solitary retreat. Sachen entered a meditation retreat of Manjushri that lasted about six months, remaining in very strict seclusion without speaking to anyone. During this retreat, he beheld a resplendent vision of Manjushri, seated on an upright throne with hands in the teaching mudra, in the posture in which the future buddha Maitreya traditionally appears. Manjushri was flanked on either side by the bodhisattvas Akshayamati and Pratibhanakuta.

As Sachen remained in meditation, rapt with the vision of Manjushri and the bodhisattvas, suddenly the deity Manjushri himself uttered the teaching in four lines that has come to be known as Parting from the Four Attachments (*Zhenpa Zhidrel*).

If you are attached to this life,
you are not a person of Dharma.
If you are attached to cyclic existence,
you do not have renunciation.
If you are attached to your own purpose,
you do not have bodhichitta.
If grasping arises,
you do not have the view.

After receiving these teachings, Sachen, being versed in the scriptures in general and the Prajñaparamita, or Perfection of Wisdom, teachings in particular, immediately understood that these four lines contained the meaning of all the sutra teachings. He saw that all of the teachings of the Mahayana vehicle of the transcendental perfections (*paramitayana*) were contained in these four lines. Sachen understood that the import of these verses was both vast and profound.

Having carefully contemplated the meaning of these four lines, Sachen came to realize that they encompassed not only the sutra teachings but in fact held the very essence of both the sutra and tantra teachings, of both the exoteric and the esoteric teachings of the Buddha. They revealed the quintessence of the complete teachings of the Buddha. And so these four themes would be widely expounded and propagated as Zhenpa Zhidrel, or Parting from the Four Attachments. Thus, this teaching has been revered as a key oral instruction and has become the basis for all of the mind training teachings in the Sakya tradition. Being able to truly understand the meaning of these four lines will bring about great realization.

As a result of his experiencing the pure vision of Manjushri, Sachen Kunga Nyingpo is regarded as an emanation of Manjushri himself. This is the origin of the third excellent name by which the Khon family is known, "the miraculous hereditary lineage of Manjushri."

Sachen's mother sent him to learn at the great seminary of Rong Ngurmik, which is famed for having been attended by as many as 10,000 students studying Buddhist philosophy. While he was studying there, one day back at Sakya there appeared a mysterious messenger riding a white horse who announced that Sachen had fallen seriously ill from smallpox. Tradition has it that this messenger was an emanation of Kardud, a protector who is associated with the meditation deity Vajrakilaya, whereas the main protectors of the Sakya school are Vajrapanjara and Four-faced Mahakala. The divine messenger said, "How could you people leave him in such an afflicted state, suffering a terrible illness? Why don't you go and care for him?"

Greatly saddened by this news, Sachen's mother went immediately back to Rong Ngurmik to see him, accompanied by many people from Sakya. She wept at the sight of Sachen in his illness. Sachen was also troubled, but his mother consoled him, saying that he need not be sad, since even if he were to die, it would be fine, as he had been spending his life well, studying in the company of 10,000 monks. Sachen's mother was always very skillful in consoling and encouraging him, even when he was stricken with severe illness.

In addition to these events that describe how Sachen became known as the emanation of the bodhisattva Manjushri, there are also other indications that have led to his being regarded an emanation of the bodhisattva Avalokiteshvara, or Chenrezig. Once, a person who had faith in Sachen insisted that unless Sachen showed some sign of being Avalokiteshvara, that person would kill himself. Under pressure from this threat, Sachen wiped his right hand on his robe and then displayed his palm, where the disciple was able to see an eye appearing clearly there. In his thousand-armed form, Avalokiteshvara has an eye in the palm of each of his thousand hands, so this was indeed a clear sign that he was an emanation of Avalokiteshvara. There are many remarkable stories from the life of Sachen that demonstrate his identity as a sublime being.

Sachen gave a detailed commentary on these verses spoken by Manjushri. This was later passed down from Sachen to two of his sons, Sonam Tsemo and Dragpa Gyaltsen, the second and third of the five founding masters of the Sakya tradition. Sachen's eldest son, Sonam Tsemo, studied in the great monastic university of Sangphu, one of the earliest monastic universities to be established in Tibet. He became an excellent scholar, renowned in Tibet and India; it was even said that north of the river Ganges, in India, there was no one who had not heard of Sonam Tsemo.

Sonam Tsemso requested that his younger brother Drakpa Gyaltsen remain at home so that he could travel and pursue his studies. Drakpa Gyaltsen remained at Sakya, staying close to his father and teacher, Sachen, as his attendant, all the while studying and practicing constantly. While Sonam Tsemo became a scholar, his younger brother Drakpa Gyaltsen chose the path of a reclusive meditator.

Drakpa Gyaltsen became a great accomplished master, a *siddha* who showed many signs, such as leaving his vajra and bell suspended in space during his prayers. He persevered with great diligence in the practice of meditation, and thus he, too, was granted the vision of Manjushri, just as his father had been. It was as a result of this that he displayed many signs of accomplishment. Once, when Drakpa Gyaltsen was in the company of many esteemed masters, vajra holders, he outdid them all by flying up from their midst into the sky.

Drakpa Gyaltsen truly became a crown jewel among all the Tibetan Buddhist masters. He possessed great experiential realizations, such as those he condensed into a song illuminating the four lines spoken by Manjushri to his father, Sachen. It is this "Song of Experience" (*nyam yang*), which was sung to explain the four verses of Parting from the Four Attachments, that we will comment on in the course of these teachings.

Drakpa Gyaltsen passed these teachings on to others, in particular, to his nephew and disciple Sakya Pandita, the fourth founding master of the Sakya tradition. Sakya Pandita, the unexcelled scholar of Tibet, master of the five outer and five inner sciences, is himself universally regarded as an emanation of Manjushri. In his pure vision that arose out of meditation, Sakya Pandita saw his uncle Drakpa Gyaltsen inseparable in form from Manjushri. While Sakya Pandita is himself definitely an emanation of the bodhisattva Manjushri, the fact that he was able to ascend to such extraordinary heights in study and meditative realization is also due to the blessings of the profound guru yoga practice, which he meditated on in relation to his uncle and guru, Drakpa Gyaltsen.

Sakya Pandita is renowned as the first Tibetan scholar whose works on Buddhism were so significant that they were translated into Indian languages. As a distinguished scholar in all fields of science and study, Sakya Pandita drew the attention not only of the people of Tibet but of all neighboring countries as well. Their kings wished Sakya Pandita to become their royal preceptor. One ruler who accepted him as a teacher was the Mongol khan, Koden. The Mongol ruler exercised great military power, but he was very inspired by the spiritual might of the Tibetan Buddhist practitioners. The khan wished to receive spiritual guidance from the great Tibetan masters, and as Sakya Pandita was the most acclaimed Tibetan master of those times, the khan invited him to China to spread the Buddhist teachings.

During one discourse, Sakya Pandita presented an example of the rarity of gaining a precious human rebirth, saying that this was rarer than hair on a turtle. Advised by his ministers, the emperor replied that he had a turtle shell that had a single hair, several inches long, growing from it. When the ministers showed this to Sakya Pandita in an effort to discredit his analogy, he immediately explained that this was no ordinary turtle. He recalled the tales of Shakyamuni Buddha's earlier rebirths as 500 "impure" life forms, saying that this turtle shell was that of Buddha Shakyamuni's birth as a turtle. He said that this shell was exceedingly rare and showed them many marks of enlightenment depicted on the shell, which they had not recognized. He scolded them, saying they were no more clever than animals.

The khan found this difficult to accept and decided to test Sakya Pandita's level of accomplishment. In those days, the magicians of China were highly skilled in the creation of magical illusions. To the north of the palace was a small lake with an island where the khan instructed his magicians to create an illusory palace. He ordered the magicians to invite Sakya Pandita into the palace and then, as soon as he had entered, to cause the palace to vanish.

Sakya Pandita consented to enter the magical palace, but a moment before he set foot on the island, he spontaneously composed a verse of consecration, saying, "By the immutable blessings of the Buddha's body, may this be auspicious..." and so on. Having spoken these words, he consecrated that place, as a result of which the magician who had created the palace was unable to cause it to disappear. Even to this day there are ruins of that miraculous palace that can be seen in the ancient city of Lhanchou in the Ganxu Province of southwestern China.

Sakya Pandita spent most of his later years living in the khan's palace and imparting teachings and so was unable to come back to Tibet. His devotees in Tibet repeatedly sent messengers, requesting him to return. In response, Sakya Pandita wrote the work known as *The Noble Path of the Great Enlightened Ones* and sent it to Tibet, saying that even if he were to come there, he had no more to teach them beyond what was contained in that book. He said that due to his age he was unable to journey to Tibet but that they should practice the teachings he had composed for them. Having written this last work, he passed away at the khan's palace in Lhanchou.

Sakya Pandita transmitted the teachings on Parting from the Four Attachments to his disciple Nupa Rikzin Drak, and also wrote a commentary on these instructions. The teachings continued to be handed down through outstanding teachers such as Lama Dampa Sonam Gyaltsen, who became a very celebrated teacher of many Buddhist masters.

Of the five founding masters of Sakya, all of whom are in the lineage of Parting from the Four Attachments, the fifth was the nephew of Sakya Pandita, whose name was Chogyal Phagpa. He became spiritual teacher to the emperor of China, the Mongol ruler Kublai Khan. *Phagpa* means "one who excels." Even at the age of eight years, he was able to understand profound texts such as the *Hevajra Tantra*. He quickly knew such books by heart and would give very detailed expositions on any number of teachings from a very young age. As an offering of gratitude for receiving teachings from him, the Chinese emperor Sechen Khan granted Chogyal Phagpa authority over the whole of Tibet. Following his example, later Chinese emperors continued the tradition of revering the descendants of the Khon lineage as their spiritual preceptors.

In a later generation, when the Chinese emperor of that time inquired about the status of the family lineage of Sakya Pandita in Tibet, the ministers responded that it had continued and was currently headed by the great lord Zangpo Pal. Since there was a perceived danger of the hereditary line of the Khon family being broken, the emperor decreed that the throne holder of Sakya, Zangpo Pal, should have seven wives. This was to ensure that the family Dharma lineage would not be broken but would continue to carry on the legacy of the teachings of the forefathers. Having been instructed by the emperor to marry as many as seven wives, Zangpo Pal fathered fifteen sons, securing the future of the tradition.

As the eldest of the fifteen sons of Zangpo Pal, Lama Dampa Sonam Gyaltsen was born into illustrious circumstances. Lama Dampa, being a devout practitioner, only very reluctantly accepted the position of authority that fell to him as representative of the Khon family. He felt that it was not a responsibility that he, as a monk, should be willing to undertake, and in time he retired, leaving his hereditary duties to his younger brothers.

Lama Dampa Sonam Gyaltsen withdrew to Samye Monastery to engage in more serious meditation retreats. Since Samye is the holy seat of Guru Padmasambhava, the founder of Buddhism in Tibet, Lama Dampa felt that he should stay there and revive and restore the practices and lineages that had been established there hundreds of years earlier. Thus, Lama Dampa came to be known as Lama Samyepa, spending much of his later life in the restoration of Samye Monastery. As he was such a reputed scholar, there were no important masters of his time who did not become his disciples.

Lama Dampa Sonam Gyaltsen had many famous disciples who excelled in the various Buddhist traditions and views, such as the Vinaya, the Prajñaparamita, or Perfection of Wisdom teachings, Madhyamaka philosophy, and so on. Even the sublime master of the Nyingma tradition, Longchen Rabjam, was a disciple of Lama Dampa. Longchen Rabjam actually inherited the name of Lama Samyepa from Lama Dampa, as he carried on the revival of Samye initiated by Lama Dampa Sonam Gyaltsen. All of the greatest masters of the Buddhist traditions of Tibet were his disciples, and for this reason Lama Dampa may be seen as the root of the non-sectarian (*rime*) tradition within Tibetan Buddhism. However, the term "non-sectarian" came into usage only at the time of Jamyang Khyentse Wangpo (1820–92).

Recently, in the era of the Thirteenth Dalai Lama, there were two great masters from the traditional seats of the Khon family, one from the Phuntsog palace and one from the Drolma palace, who were fully accomplished, having gained their realizations through the practice of the meditation deity Vajrakilaya. Their descendants in the following generation, two of whom were the father and the paternal uncle of the present Sakya Trizin, showed similar accomplishments, such as the overflowing of the ritual vessel (*kapala*) and the appearance of auspicious patterns in the sand mandala of initiation.

These teachings have come down to the present day, most recently through my root master Dampa Rinpoche, Zhenpen Nyingpo, who like his predecessors was a greatly accomplished master. These are just some of the teachers in the tradition of Parting from the Four Attachments. We are fortunate to have an unbroken lineage of the oral transmission of this teaching and its commentary reaching us through a succession of such highly realized masters. Although I may not personally have any blessings to impart, the fact that the teachings came from holy enlightened masters means that the transmission itself still contains the blessings it is intended to transmit to disciples.

When we speak of the different Dharma lineages, they are distinguished from one another on the basis of their historical background. This background includes the way in which the masters of that tradition gained realization, as well as the particular practices upon which their accomplishment was based. In order to increase our faith in the teachings and lineages with which we have made a connection, it is important to trace the validity of the teachings and the authenticity of the teachers who have transmitted them. This is why we have dwelt at some length on the history of the lineage and particularly of several of its masters.

Though there are many commentaries on the four lines of Parting from the Four Attachments, among them all, Drakpa Gyaltsen's commentary is especially beneficial for practitioners, as it is a song of spiritual experience. Sakya Pandita wrote annotations to Drakpa Gyaltsen's song, and our present root text includes these annotations by Sakya Pandita. Drakpa Gyaltsen meditated deeply upon these teachings, and whatever realization resulted from this is spontaneously expressed in the words of his song. Drakpa Gyaltsen's commentary is what is known as a *nyam yang,* a melody of meditative experience. Drakpa Gyaltsen's song is just like those of the great yogi Milarepa, as it is based on his experiential realization of the practice of meditation.

Milarepa often sang when conversing with his disciples, expressing the profound understanding he had gained of loving kindness and compassion, of emptiness and the nature of mind. His songs became literature of the greatest spiritual inspiration, motivating countless beings on the Dharma path. Drakpa Gyaltsen had many realizations similar to those of Milarepa, and like Milarepa, he passed these realizations on in the form of songs that later became sets of instructions.

Milarepa's songs, such as *The Hundred Thousand Songs of Milarepa,* are said to have arisen naturally out of the deep experience of meditation. They were spoken or sung extemporaneously, without the need to prepare their content intellectually. Rather, they were evoked spontaneously from realizations that arose through his practice. In the same way, this song of Drakpa Gyaltsen is the uncontrived expression of his own experience, gained while meditating on the four lines of Manjushri and written down at the request of one of his disciples. It is very moving to hear the experiential songs of great yogis.

Drakpa Gyaltsen held this teaching on Parting from the Four Attachments in the highest regard. Through meditation, he gained vast and profound realizations and produced the first written commentary on these four verses of the bodhisattva Manjushri. Other early commentaries on the four lines are by Nupa Rikzin Drak, Sakya Pandita, Ngorchen Kunga Zangpo, Gorampa Sonam Senge, and many others.

Ngorchen Kunga Zangpo's nephew wrote an extensive commentary on Parting from the Four Attachments based on Drakpa Gyaltsen's song and Sakya Pandita's annotations. This is the commentary traditionally used to impart the teachings in their elaborate form over a period of seven days. Since we have less time, I will give these teachings based on the song of Drakpa Gyaltsen. As Drakpa Gyaltsen was a greatly realized meditator, his expressions are direct, simple, and to the point. Though his song of experience is succinct, it contains all the key meanings concealed within the four lines.

2. Attachment to This Life

꧁

THERE IS A TRADITION that describes the manner in which teachings can be given. The first way of teaching is that of a person of high status, one such as His Holiness Sakya Trizin, who, while sitting on a high throne with dignity and stature, may present a grand and eloquent exposition. The second manner of teaching is the scholarly discourse. The scholar will not only discuss the topic but will support the teachings and their contents by providing extensive commentaries from the sutras as well as from later works by various learned masters.

The third type of teaching presents experiential realizations gained through meditation practice. Jetsun Drakpa Gyaltsen's writings and spontaneous songs belong to this category, as they are based on his deep personal experience and insights, such as those he had while meditating on these four lines of Manjushri. Drakpa Gyaltsen's commentary is not written in the erudite language of scholars; rather, its tone is experiential. His are words of direct realization rather than scholarly composition. Since Drakpa Gyaltsen had gained great certainty and confidence in the teaching through his own realization of the meaning of the four lines, this served as a guarantee that they would in the future be used as the root verses for elaborate and comprehensive teachings by scholars.

High-ranking learned masters would thus later be able to give eloquent discourses based on these four lines, spending an entire week explaining the meaning of both sutra and tantra based on them. It was Ngorchen Kunga Zangpo and his successors who instituted the tradition of expounding upon these four lines for up to a week at a time. The framework of the four lines became a means of communicating all the fundamental teachings of the Buddha. Thus, we can see how these verses came to be used as a root text for scholars as well as for accomplished meditators.

This work of Drakpa Gyaltsen is eminently practical, since it actually has the power to instill realizations in the minds of practitioners. It is capable of evoking realization as it is spoken, listened to, and learned. It is for this reason that we will use his precious words to understand the meaning of Manjushri's four-line teaching.

> May the kind teachers and compassionate tantric deities
> In whom I take refuge from my heart
> Please bestow blessings upon me.

Jetsun Drakpa Gyaltsen's work begins with two verses. The first is a salutation and supplication, and this is followed by a verse promising to compose this song expressing the meaning of the four lines. These opening verses are followed by the main part of the teaching, and he ends his song with the dedication of merit. In this way, Drakpa Gyaltsen divides his song into four sections.

In the first line, he pays homage to his most kind root guru, meaning the spiritual masters, and to the most compassionate deities, meaning the tantric meditation deities, the *yidams*. Drakpa Gyaltsen is requesting the blessings of his spiritual masters, of the meditation deities, and of the Three Jewels in order that he may succeed in sharing his realization. He takes refuge and pays homage from the depth of his heart and seeks the blessings of the gurus and deities so that his mindstream will be consecrated and that whatever blessings he receives will be articulated in this work. This is to ensure that what is shared will be fruitful and will bestow great benefits.

This is a firmly established tradition, whereby authors of Buddhist treatises always begin by paying homage to the great teachers. It is stated in the writings of Sakya Pandita that authentic works must bear at least one line, if not an entire verse, paying homage to the masters under whom the author of the text studied. This is to show that it is not something the author has produced on his own but is based on the blessings he has received from the lineage holders.

It is unnecessary to act without [regard for] Dharma.
As for the manner of accomplishing Dharma,
I request you to listen to this instruction on
Parting from the Four Attachments.

*Thus, the invocation and promise to explain the teaching have
been made by the author.*

The supplication is followed by the second verse, the statement of
purpose for which the author is composing the treatise. Here, Drakpa
Gyaltsen resolves to offer this teaching, saying that it is unnecessary
for one to persist in deeds that do not accord with the Dharma teachings. He is saying that in order to carry out activities that are in accord
with the Dharma, we should listen to the instructions on Parting from
the Four Attachments.

This is a prelude to introducing the first line of Bodhisattva Manjushri, which refers to not being attached to the affairs of this life.
Drakpa Gyaltsen sings that the principles he outlines in his song are
appropriate only for those who wish to find themselves in harmony
with the teachings of authentic spirituality. He is indicating how
unsuitable this text will be for those who are engaged in activities that
contradict the spiritual precepts.

What this teaching is saying is that to be able to remain stable on the
path of the Dharma, whether one is studying, meditating, or expounding the teachings, it is completely necessary that one's own person
should truly conform to and reflect the spirit of the Dharma. Squan-
dering our lives engaging in activities that contradict Dharma principles goes against the very spirit of the teachings.

Those who wish to engage in the authentic Dharma have a great
need to hear and understand the instructions on parting from, or free-
ing oneself from, the four attachments indicated by Manjushri himself. The sincere practitioner may follow these instructions, which will
help them to proceed along the path. Remaining true to the spirit of
the Dharma means to be neither tarnished nor corrupted by any of
the four traps, or four kinds of attachment, revealed by Manjushri.

In order to correctly follow the path of Dharma, Drakpa Gyaltsen
says, one ought to listen to and comprehend the meaning of these

teachings. He asks that we be truly mindful, wakeful, as we listen to his song of experience. Those who wish to avoid many potential pitfalls need to listen to and be heedful of the meaning of Parting from the Four Attachments. Specifically, Drakpa Gyaltsen may be addressing his noted disciple Kar Shakya Drak, who is thought to have requested this song.

Thus, the first two lines of Drakpa Gyaltsen's song are the supplication, the seeking of blessings, and the second two lines are the promise to write the text. This is in accordance with the tradition of Buddhist scholars of never failing to place a supplication at the beginning of any work and always following this with a statement of the purpose for which they are composing the treatise.

To summarize the meanings we will explore in this teaching, we will see that parting, or liberating oneself, from the four attachments means to let go of attachment to one's welfare in this life alone. It means to free oneself from being attached to worldly existence. It means to part from the attachment to one's own selfish purposes. Ultimately, it means to release grasping or fixating on a conceptual view or rigid dogma that one believes to be "supreme truth."

(1)   If you are attached to this life,
                       you are not a person of Dharma.

First, for non-attachment to this life,
You must put aside the non-Dharma person's [manner of]
Practicing moral conduct, hearing, contemplation, and
     meditation,
Which are performed for the sake of this life.

To begin with, moral conduct is explained as endowing
     [one] with
The root for accomplishing the higher realms,
The ladder for attaining liberation,
And the antidote by which one abandons suffering.

Though there is no method [for gaining liberation]
Without moral conduct,

The moral conduct of one attached to this life is endowed with
The root for accomplishing the eight worldly concerns,
Denigration of [those possessing] inferior moral conduct,
Jealousy toward the righteous,
Hypocrisy in one's own moral conduct,
And the seed for attaining the lower realms.
Put aside this false moral conduct.

First, Manjushri declares that one who is attached to this life is not yet an authentically spiritual person. To become a genuine practitioner of the spiritual path, it is necessary not to be overly attached to this life. Jetsun Drakpa Gyaltsen's words do not elaborate in great detail on Manjushri's words. They speak very succinctly, in the kind of teaching known as "practical instructions" (*mar tri*). This style of teaching is similar to when you are learning to read, and your teacher guides you slowly and carefully, pointing at each syllable and guiding you through the words one by one. Drakpa Gyaltsen says that he will accept the task of concisely revealing the pith instructions, the essential keys necessary for practice. Drakpa Gyaltsen's words strike the vital topics, unerringly finding the "pressure points" that must be "pressed" in order to produce the desired effects.

The basis for what Drakpa Gyaltsen wishes to convey regarding this first line of Manjushri is inspired by, and elaborates upon, a famous two-line quote from the *Abhidharmakosha* by the Indian pandita Vasubandhu. Vasubandhu tells us that one abides by the ethical precepts and contemplates the teachings in order to enter into profound meditation. He is informing us that one should follow a process of first observing the precepts of ethical conduct, and then studying and learning until one gains some understanding and conviction as to the truth of the teachings. Once understanding has taken root in this way, this knowledge needs to be applied through the practice of meditation so that one may develop one's own genuine experience. We will examine in detail each of these three: ethical conduct, study, and meditation.

In the manner favored by the Sakya tradition of imparting teachings, the teachings are repeated many times. Ideally, it is best to go over the complete teachings four times. Repetition enables us to discover new significance and depth of meaning within the teachings. One may receive the teachings, and then go home and reflect and meditate on them. When they are repeated the next day along with additional explanations, the transmission is considered more complete and efficacious. For this reason, we will go over the main points of these teachings more than once.

First, let us look into what it means to part from the attachment to one's welfare in this life. If one is attached to the purposes of this life, then whatever practices of Dharma one may attempt, whether of morality, study, or meditation, these practices will become contaminated by this attachment. Due to this contamination, our practices fail to become causes that will qualify us as a genuine spiritual practitioner, as a Dharma person. On the other hand, one who studies, contemplates, and meditates without investment in, and attachment to, this life is certainly one who practices according to the true spirit of the Dharma.

All three of these trainings, those of ethical conduct, study, and meditation, may be viewed in terms of two broad themes: authentic or genuine spiritual practice on the one hand, and inauthentic or superficial practice on the other. Whether or not our practice of ethics, study, and meditation is valid or invalid depends on whether or not we are attached to our welfare in this life alone.

Ideally, these three elements of practice must work together, with study and meditation developing out of the firm foundation of upright ethical conduct. Study and meditation will fully flourish out of this foundation of ethical behavior, just like the waxing of the moon. Thus, it is stated in the *Abhidharmakosha* that having relied upon the discipline of ethical conduct, one should then properly enter into the practice of study and meditation.

Whatever you study, it is necessary to examine, analyze, and contemplate it in order to clarify all doubts and questions. The depth of conviction that you gain from such study and contemplation remains very deeply seated within you, setting a firm basis for further realizations. Having clarified all your major doubts and questions, it is necessary to continue to progress and deepen your understanding by following the practice of meditation.

To study and to contemplate what one has learned is very important, but these two can only progress if one engages in meditation practice.

Thus, the importance of each of these three—moral conduct, study, and meditation—cannot be underestimated. If one practices these free of attachment to this life, the benefits are enormous. But to pursue these while seeking worldly attainments means one will not receive the benefits that would be gained by a genuine spiritual practitioner. For this reason, it will be best if you abandon any inauthentic approaches to ethical discipline, study, and meditation.

Whether one studies or meditates, if one is actually just interested in this life's welfare, wishing to appear to others as a great practitioner, then this is artificial practice. In fact, such an approach defeats the whole purpose of following the Dharma. Wouldn't it be better not to go through so much trouble for nothing? On the other hand, properly motivated study definitely dispels mental darkness, and meditation approached correctly certainly deepens spiritual realization.

With these considerations in mind, Jetsun Drakpa Gyaltsen begins by emphasizing the importance of distinguishing between the proper and the improper practice of ethical conduct, study, and meditation, since all three of these are easily affected by attachments to this life. He is asking, "If it is true that one attached to this life's purposes alone is not yet a spiritual person, then how does one proceed to practice Dharma and remain free of these attachments?"

Drakpa Gyaltsen suggests that to understand this, it is necessary to know that whatever kind of practice one may do, there are two possibilities: the practice may be genuine and in accord with the Dharma, or it may be artificial. One must first distinguish between these two so that one will know what to adopt and practice, and what to abandon and renounce. It is said that when a person practices ethics, study, and meditation simply due to attachments, his or her practice of these will only be the cause for accumulating the eight worldly dharmas, the eight worldly concerns. The term "eight worldly concerns" refers to being attached to gain and loss, pleasure and pain, praise and blame, and fame and infamy.

Let us examine in more depth the question of authentic ethical conduct. Even though one may take vows to observe moral precepts, keeping precepts should not be used as a means of adorning oneself. This means that the purpose of ethical conduct is not to meet the needs of this life, enhance one's name and reputation, or gain honor and devotion from others. If we attempt to practice the Dharma while we are caught up in such superficial considerations, this is artificial or insincere Dharma practice.

If we are afflicted by the eight worldly concerns, our practice will suffer accordingly. There are signs by which we can distinguish if our practice of moral discipline has been rendered inauthentic in this way. One definite sign of this is that we will look down on those "transgressors" whom we deem not to measure up to our standards; we will feel jealous toward those who appear more stainless in their conduct than we ourselves do; and in relation to our own person, our practice will become a cause for arrogance.

Ethical discipline (*tsultrim*) is like our legs, which must be strong in order to traverse the path of the Dharma and acquire all necessary qualities along the way. If one lacks this strength due to corrupted conduct, one becomes like a crippled person who must struggle desperately to reach his or her destination, if it is ever reached at all! For this reason, it is necessary to practice discipline so that it is not defiled by the eight worldly concerns. Drakpa Gyaltsen requests his listeners to distinguish between the pure and the corrupted forms of morality.

Buddhist practitioners have three types of ordinary vows: refuge vows, novice monastic vows (*getsul*), and the vows of full ordination. One who has received the vows of refuge should keep the five precepts of a lay practitioner. A novice monk or nun adopts and observes these five vows, which are expanded into ten root vows that they are to maintain. A fully ordained monk has 253 vows to uphold.

Whatever discipline one undertakes to restrain harmful, unwholesome activities of body, speech, and mind, whether as a lay practitioner or as one with ordination, if one observes the precepts without any hypocrisy or phoniness, then this will form the basis for present as well as ultimate happiness for oneself. Discipline earns us happiness in this life as well as higher forms of rebirth in the future and sows the seeds of liberation from samsara. However, it is necessary that we should follow the precepts without any thought of the eight worldly concerns. One who keeps the vows very carefully according to the instructions will receive many great benefits from doing so. There is immense positive value in keeping the vows of moral discipline.

For example, consider someone who upholds one of the three types of vows, such as the ten vows of a lay practitioner (*upasaka*) or the thirty-six vows of the female novice practitioner or the 253 vows of the fully ordained monk. It is important that whatever vows one may keep, they should not be kept out of intentions arising from attachment to this life, such as gaining name, fame, status, special titles with which to flatter oneself, or anything else that may serve to enhance one's self-importance. To maintain moral precepts simply in order to acquire worldly possessions for one's own welfare in this life goes against the spirit of Dharma, the spirit of non-attachment to the affairs of this life.

Restraining one's body, speech, and mind from wrongdoing and engaging in virtue is absolutely necessary for attaining liberation. If one is able to engage in the ten wholesome deeds of body, speech, and mind, they become the direct causes of happiness. Whether or not one gains at least a human rebirth in the next life depends solely on the virtuous deeds one is able to accumulate in this life.

The ten virtuous deeds are the basis for moral and ethical conduct. The ten virtuous deeds come about naturally once one refrains from the following ten actions: Refraining from (1) taking life, (2) taking what is not given, and (3) sexual misconduct produces in turn the three virtuous actions of body. Refraining from (4) lying, (5) slander, (6) harsh speech, and (7) idle speech produces the four virtuous deeds of speech. Refraining from (8) envy, (9) ill will, and (10) holding wrong views gives rise to the three virtuous deeds of mind.

One refrains from these ten non-virtuous actions while strengthening one's conduct with positive actions, such as saving life instead of killing, giving to the poor instead of stealing, and so on. All virtues, such as generosity, patience, and ethical discipline, give rise to wholesome deeds that result in happiness. If the ethical precepts relating to the ten virtuous deeds are practiced and maintained in this lifetime, they become like a ladder upon which one will be able to ascend to the citadel of liberation. Virtue is an unavoidable requisite on the path of Dharma.

Pure moral discipline means to practice according to the instructions of the tradition. Authentic ethical conduct means that one has the excellent intention of keeping one's discipline until reaching enlightenment, with the motivation of benefiting all sentient beings. The genuine practice of ethics offers a solace that actually pacifies and "cools down" one's being, making it possible to relinquish whatever sufferings may torment us. Ethical discipline acts to soothe our suffering and gives us a strength of faith, devotion, and self-discipline that otherwise would be lacking. This is why it is so essential to persevere in the practice of ethics.

If ethics and virtue are practiced properly, not only does this serve as an antidote for all the miseries and dissatisfaction one encounters in this life, but it also guarantees a higher rebirth in the future. It leads directly to the "hearer"(*sravaka*) and the "solitary awakened one" (*pratyekabuddha*) stages of the attainment of nirvana, and to the possibility of attaining ultimate enlightenment (*samyaksambuddha*). Likewise, the Mahayana practices of bodhichitta, the mind of enlightenment, depend upon a foundation of sound discipline. In fact, without this ethical basis, one cannot really make any further stable progress in spiritual realization. On the other hand, one who possesses such discipline as a basis can then progress quite rapidly.

Whatever practices one may later undertake, their success depends entirely on how stable one's foundation of virtue is, regardless of whether one follows the conduct of a layperson or that of a fully ordained monk or nun. A practitioner must have this foundation as the basis from which all subsequent study and practice can genuinely progress. This prepares one's being to be like fertile soil; it is out of this soil that all of the other seeds, those of listening, contemplating, and meditating, may germinate.

Without this foundation, whatever study and practice one may do will tend to be contrived or superficial and will not yield the fruits of realization and enlightenment. Jetsun Drakpa Gyaltsen says that in fact one might as well abandon whatever study, contemplation, and meditation one has undertaken if virtuous conduct is absent. He asks, "Would it not be better to simply give up artificial Dharma practice?"

Why does Drakpa Gyaltsen say this? If we do not keep our ethical commitments properly, it is quite impossible to be born even as a human or as a god, since the central cause for acquiring such births is self-discipline. If one practices giving or generosity, this will definitely lead to a birth in which one is wealthy, but by itself it does not even guarantee us a rebirth as a human or a god. Due to the practice of generosity in previous lifetimes that nonetheless lacked a corresponding practice of ethics, one may be born as an animal, such as a monkey, and still be surrounded by gold or treasures. Generosity alone might allow us to enjoy a wonderfully abundant existence as a monkey in the forest, but without disciplined virtue one will probably not progress further!

From this example, it can be understood that without the observance of ethical conduct, the practice of the other five transcendental perfections (*paramitas*) will not guarantee higher rebirth. The practice of ethical discipline is indispensable, as it is only on the basis of a higher rebirth, such as that of a human being, that one is able to attain liberation. This is why it is said that authentic morality is both the antidote to suffering and the staircase to liberation.

Thus, Drakpa Gyaltsen tells us that the practice of ethics is something one simply cannot do without, whether it be solely for the purpose of attaining the mundane achievements of samsara, or whether it is in order to attain supramundane qualities and ultimate liberation. Even for one who practices as a layperson, upholding five or ten precepts, if the precepts are maintained genuinely and without hypocrisy, then this very practice is exactly the root cause necessary for attaining higher rebirth.

It is said that the accumulation of virtuous, meritorious deeds in one's present lifetime is indispensable for gaining a precious human rebirth again in the future. This means that the fact that we have attained a precious human rebirth at this time is the direct karmic result of having maintained moral precepts in a previous lifetime. When one refrains from the ten non-virtuous deeds in this lifetime, it ensures that one's future births will be conducive to the pursuit of enlightenment.

However, when it comes to the manner in which one acts upon one's ethical values, some practitioners try to keep up their discipline while at the same time maintaining quite a bit of attachment to this life. This means that they continue to harbor intentions of gaining temporary benefits during their present lifetime, seeking praise, honor, respect, and so on. This type of morality, mixed with worldly motives and pursuits, is what is known as impure morality.

How does impure morality function in the experience of a practitioner? One afflicted by the eight worldly concerns will only be able to partially follow the precepts, due to improper motivation and misguided intentions. This corrupts one's own behavior while at the same time making one judgmental, critical, and even jealous of the conduct of others.

There are many excellent examples that help us to recognize these kinds of problems. One example would be that a person might maintain a set of vows but at the same time make disparaging remarks such as, "Oh, those people have taken vows but they don't keep them carefully. They certainly have let themselves down. However, my own conduct is really exemplary." Faulting the behavior of others through demeaning comments while at the same time finding ways to praise one's own behavior is one fine example that indicates a defiled or insincere practice of ethics.

Another variation on how this impure form of morality reveals itself is that not only will one tend to look down on "transgressors" who are deemed inferior, but one may also regard those who keep superior discipline with a jealous attitude. One will be unable to restrain oneself from making comments such as, "Well, I suppose he keeps his vows intact, but he hasn't really studied or meditated."

In more extreme cases, practitioners of artificial morality may actually become very jealous of others who are known to keep strict moral discipline. They may say, "Oh, he or she seems to be very true to the precepts, but...," and then go on to list the person's supposed defects, such as greed and so on, proceeding to slander him or her. Although the discipline of the one they are criticizing may be very admirable, the superficial practitioner may find himself unable to tolerate that worthy person and feel compelled to look for faults in the other person's affairs.

A further degeneration of this type of attitude is that one may notice someone who makes small errors in the observance of their vows and will try to pinpoint the person's faults, even speaking of him or her sarcastically in the presence of others. One may try to place doubts in the minds of people who would otherwise respect the person due to his or her faithful adherence to the precepts. One whose morality is artificial is always looking for an excuse to put someone else down. He or she will always find something to criticize. Such a person will be much more concerned with judging the conduct of others than with guarding and protecting their own conduct. People like this will never find anyone to inspire their pursuit of virtue but will at the same time never fail to find someone to disparage. These are the sorts of results that come from the insincere practice of ethics, and we would do well to avoid them.

These kinds of attitudes we have mentioned so far all arise toward those who actually observe precepts. In addition, it is clear that one whose discipline is artificial, due to attachment to this life alone, will be very critical of others who do not observe any discipline. Such persons may be very judgmental and condescending toward those who make even small mistakes in their behavior. They will tend to chastise others for the terrible weight of their sins. They will be neither understanding nor forgiving toward the accused transgressors, since in reality their own moral conduct is practiced in order to attract respect, gain, and happiness for themselves in this life alone. All of these are examples of the sorts of attitudes that may arise in relation to others when our discipline lacks pure motivation and intent.

Now we are also given examples of the kinds of faults that will be experienced in our own observance of the precepts if our motives are less than sincere. What happens to us in this case is that our own practice suffers from hypocrisy. This is another very common way impure morality manifests. An example of this kind of hypocrisy that we may be familiar with is when people keep pure ethical conduct while in the company of others, but when others are absent, they may do whatever they wish without any concern for their discipline. Those who practice impure ethics may make a show of virtuous conduct in front of others even though they are not actually maintaining the discipline. This is because they are very worried about how others perceive them, about how they appear to others. This is inauthentic practice, as it is under the power of the eight worldly dharmas.

For instance, if one is practicing the hypocritical variety of ethical conduct, one may act in the presence of others as if one never touches alcohol. But then, when no one else is around, one may enthusiastically drink up! Or an ordained person may say, "Oh, I never eat after midday." But when no one is around, that person will eat their fill, morning or night. One who practices moral conduct for this world alone will accumulate in this way a stockpile of hypocrisy. Such "discipline" is in reality more of a cause for rebirth in the lower realms than for

liberation. It is only if one's practice of morality is genuine and pure
—that is to say, free from hypocrisy—that it becomes a cause of happiness as well as a cause for the attainment of all the levels of enlightenment.

In fact, most people's discipline does suffer from exactly this sort of
superficiality and hypocrisy. This means that we may actually be
focused on this life's welfare, chasing after fame, honor, respect, personal gain, and so on. No matter how upright we may appear, as long
as we are ensnared in these worldly concerns, we will never become
free. Since the practice of hypocritical morality actually ends up creating causes for one to be born in the three lower realms, it should be
avoided at any cost. Practicing ethics with worldly motives is likened
to falling into a pit. Hence, it is quite useful to know these things.

There is a further dimension to consider in this regard. If one uses
one's adherence to moral conduct as a means for attracting respect,
honor, a good reputation, and personal happiness in the present lifetime, then it follows that one's practice of ethics will suffer if any
conditions contrary to these occur. Were one to lose one's honor, reputation, or other fortunate conditions, one's motives and character
might be suddenly revealed.

Whatever practice we may do, if it is according to or conditioned by
the eight worldly concerns, it is actually better for us just to abandon
it as soon as possible, as it is quite harmful. On the other hand, whatever practice we follow that is truly in accord with the Dharma instructions, we should stay with by all means. True ethics and virtue must
be completely free of the eight worldly dharmas. Would it not be better to be free of hypocrisy, especially since it serves no purpose? Jetsun
Drakpa Gyaltsen is telling us that it is necessary to give up hypocritical discipline because the only "Dharmas" served are the eight worldly
ones!

If one is jealous toward those more righteous than oneself, and if
one shows oneself to be without any sympathy toward those who are
unable to fulfill precepts of ethical conduct, while at the same time
one's own ethical discipline is riddled with deception and hypocrisy,
what is the use of behaving like this? Isn't it better to abandon pre-
tenses? Hypocritical morality can easily lead to judging and finally
abusing others, and this is certain to result in an unhappy future. If

you discover this kind of hypocrisy in yourself, give it up immediately! Drakpa Gyaltsen asserts the importance of abandoning artificial ethics because hypocrisy not only becomes the cause for one to be reborn in the lower realms in the future, but it also becomes the cause of suffering in the present life. The practice of false morality actually increases and fans the flames of suffering in this very life.

Not only is there a difference between genuine and artificial morality, there are also several varieties of moral conduct, such as those associated with physical actions, verbal behavior, and mental attitudes, and all of these may be adopted sincerely or as a mere pretense. If one wishes to be skillful in determining whether an action is moral or immoral, not only in regard to outer physical actions but also in terms of internal mental attitudes, one needs to examine whether or not one's attitudes are contrary to the spirit of true ethics.

How can we know this? There are examples that give us an idea of what to look for. For instance, if we are trying to follow the moral discipline of the body, then we should keep to and preserve even the most minor points of the prescribed physical conduct. Likewise, in regard to speech, we should not neglect even short, simple requests or instructions given by our spiritual teacher. If one overlooks them, one might instead think that such and such is only a minor thing, so it doesn't really matter; even if we are contradicting the teacher's wishes, it is possible to ignore it. If one says these kinds of things to oneself, then one is disregarding the verbal aspect of moral conduct. One who is not careful and scrupulous in following the precepts will certainly overlook minor things and so end up accumulating many negative results as a consequence of his or her negligence.

This can be illustrated by the famous story of Ellapatra. Ellapatra was a *naga* being, who in a previous lifetime had been a disciple of Buddha, an ordained monk who was following the Buddha's teaching. Over the course of Buddha's lifetime, the number of vows and precepts governing the conduct of monks increased, as Buddha added further prohibitions. One such prohibition was that a fully ordained monk should not uproot trees or pull out grass from the soil.

In his birth as a monk, Ellapatra had criticized Buddha, saying, "This is such a small thing, what is he going on about?" Disregarding Buddha's instruction, Ellapatra uprooted a tree. In the monk's next lifetime, he was born as a *naga*, or serpent, and this *naga* had a huge tree growing on top of his head. Whenever a storm or winds blew the tree, the *naga*'s brains and internal organs were completely shaken up and disrupted.

As a result of this monk's negative karma of speech, saying, "We can overlook this statement of the Buddha since it is such a small thing," he ended up creating powerful demerit. This story illustrates that one who wishes to practice ethics must be sincere as well as very careful, being conscientious and precise about even little things in order to remain true to the sense and spirit in which the precepts were originally laid out.

In addition to ethical behavior, the triad of hearing, contemplation, and meditation are also indispensable if one wishes to attain enlightenment. However, these also must be practiced in their purity in order to be effective. Just as the practice of ethics has both a genuine and an inauthentic dimension, the same is true of the triad of hearing or study, contemplation, and meditation. Once again, Drakpa Gyaltsen's point is that whatever Dharma practice one may do, if one remains attached to this life, then it is better to give it up. It will not bestow the benefits for which it is intended and instead will harm us. Rather, we should follow the proper tradition of practice as taught in the three higher trainings.

In terms of "hearing," or study, we must know how to study properly. This means not merely learning in order to show how much one knows but rather so that one may overcome one's grasping and clinging to knowledge itself. Likewise with contemplation, one should not ponder the teachings in order to impress others but should progress in the development of one's inner understanding according to the tradition. Similarly, for a meditator it is essential that one should not make a show of oneself, acting for the sake of appearances.

Just as with the adoption of ethical precepts, likewise, if we want to study, contemplate, and meditate, we must do our best to practice these purely and avoid the impure or inauthentic styles of practice. With all three of these, one should know both the pure as well as the impure aspect of each; this is what enables us to practice properly while avoiding adulterated practice. Otherwise, it may well happen that one's practice of hearing, contemplation, and meditation becomes mixed with the eight worldly concerns.

The general examples for all of these are the same, that one may find oneself to be jealous and competitive toward others who endeavor well in any of these three. Conversely, one notices oneself gossiping about others who do not practice these so well. One might say, "Oh, they don't really study, contemplate, or meditate very much. How will they ever become enlightened?" For someone who behaves in this way, their own practice will inevitably develop shortcomings.

What sort of shortcomings might someone like this be prone to experience? One example that is easy to observe is that when such a person listens to or studies some topic, something will disturb their mind. When they contemplate, some outside noise or other factors may distract them. When they practice meditation, their mind may lose its object or focus and may seem constantly to wander off somewhere else. These kinds of experiences of distraction result from impure or defiled hearing, contemplation, and meditation.

Again, in general we can observe the same sort of pattern emerging that one finds in the practice of morality. If we are jealous of those who study, contemplate, or meditate well while being condescending toward those who do not, then although we may exert ourselves in any of these, we will find that we are constantly distracted by worldly matters. This is the sign that our practice is tainted, that we have fallen into the trap of practicing according to the eight worldly concerns, and that we have failed to discriminate between authentic and inauthentic practice.

> The person who undertakes hearing and contemplation
> Is endowed with the wealth for accomplishing knowledge,
> The lamp that dispels ignorance,
> The knowledge of the path by which to guide living beings,
> And the seed of the *dharmakaya*.

Having discussed the valid and invalid application of ethical conduct in depth, let us now examine in detail this same principle in relation to the practice of studying the Dharma, which is traditionally known as "listening," or "hearing." We ought to study Dharma properly and with great intent, unstained by attachment to our own welfare and honor in this life, and with the intention to liberate ourselves from such attachments. If we learn and study in this way, then this process of study becomes the skillful means of acquiring the splendor and wealth of knowledge. One will find that one becomes truly contented through the knowledge that one has acquired.

For those who study with proper intentions, anything they may learn will serve to dispel the darkness of ignorance and confusion they may be experiencing in their own lives. This is because whatever they study, they will apply it to themselves, and this will alleviate the sufferings that afflict them. Anything such people may study will further serve to humble and ennoble them, increasing their clarity and brilliance, their knowledge and wisdom. Genuine study is the basis for attaining enlightenment, a cause for oneself finally to attain the state of *dharmakaya*, the wisdom body of truth, or reality.

If the acquisition of knowledge progresses to clear discernment and great conviction, then not only does this dispel one's own negativities and confusion, but it is also a torch that can light the way for others, guiding them to safety while helping them to avoid darkened byways. The person with knowledge and wisdom is like a torchbearer. When others stumble on in darkness, unable to find their way, the one with knowledge will be able to find the path, regardless of the circumstances. Such a person becomes an experienced and trustworthy guide, one who can help many travelers who might otherwise become lost, schooling them in what is right and what is wrong, in what to adopt and what to abandon in order to follow the path. Genuine knowledge eliminates the slumber of mental darkness, by the light that is lit within one's being through authentic study.

Those with wisdom have immense gratitude toward their spiritual masters, for in them they have found the trustworthy guide who is able to illuminate the darkness of their own ignorance and lead them to the citadel of liberation. Ordinary sentient beings who are lost on the long journey of life will not know which way to go, when to continue, or where to take a different path; they are unable to make the correct choices for themselves. Their choices may even give rise to more guilt and self-denigration, even self-loathing. A person enriched by learning and study can serve as an experienced guide in the bewildering and perilous journey of life, showing people how to simplify the complex difficulties of their lives in order to carry on with their journey.

We can all observe how a great scholar will convey clarification, understanding, and inspiration to many people. Just like a mirror that reflects clearly both oneself and one's environment, so the intelligence and wisdom gained through study can give the learned a profound understanding of themselves and their world. Through proper study, you are able to discern the ultimate nature of reality, as well as to understand the actual condition of everything and everyone around you. Proper study provides you with a mirror that allows you to perceive very clearly many things that you otherwise would have no way of knowing.

It is through hearing and study, learning about the Dharma, that one discovers the possibility of oneself becoming a buddha. Although we all have the qualities of a buddha, the seed of buddhahood, lying dormant within us, we normally do not appreciate this fact. By learning and studying the Dharma, we come to appreciate our potential, and this infuses us with a newfound feeling of hope and possibility. This can cause us to reevaluate our lives, discovering a value and meaning in life that would have remained hidden from us had we not entered into learning and study.

> Though there is no method [for gaining liberation]
> Without hearing and contemplation,
> One who hears and contemplates while attached to this life
> Is endowed with the wealth that accomplishes pride,
> Contempt for [those] inferior in hearing and contemplation,
> Jealousy toward those who possess hearing and contemplation,
> The pursuit of followers and wealth,
> And the root [causes] for attaining the lower realms.
> Put aside this hearing and contemplation [based on]
> The eight worldly concerns.

However valuable learning may be, if one studies and contemplates with worldly motives, it will bear no truly beneficial results; rather than becoming a cause for liberation, study may instead merely increase the wealth of one's arrogance. Our studies may end up educating us in how to become jealous, in how to cultivate such pride that it may seem as though we are the only one who knows anything, while everyone else is simply ignorant. Anything that is learned may serve to bloat the ego, making one pretentious and haughty. Not only will such a person's learning cause them to suffer these faults within themselves, but it will also create problems for them in terms of how they perceive others who are studying and learning.

It is said that one who has studied with the mistaken attachment to their welfare in this life alone will look down on those who have not studied as much as they have, rejecting the other persons, ignoring them, even behaving hurtfully toward them. Such a person may say, "Oh well, even though he may have done this or that, he hasn't really studied and doesn't know what he is talking about." Having put themselves on a pedestal, they are unable to see any quality whatsoever in others, blinded by their own arrogance. Their knowledge has given them license to belittle others, to find fault with others but never with themselves.

As if this is not bad enough, in relation to those learned ones who are known to have truly studied and contemplated well, such a person will actually be very jealous and will try to look for weakness in those people, saying, "Even though they may be very learned in this subject, still they are lacking in such-and-such other qualities." These kinds of attitudes are simply due to the person's own sense of insecurity and inferiority, which causes them to disparage others, whether their knowledge may be greater or less than their own. Someone like this will sow seeds of discord and feel that they must try to get people to side with them, fearful that others will not support their opinions.

The study of Buddhadharma is provided as a means for one to gain liberation, to attain enlightenment. But for one whose motives for study are suspect, their knowledge does not become the cause for liberation from cyclic existence but instead becomes the cause for them to acquire a larger entourage, a bigger following, a higher-sounding title, and a greater accumulation of wealth and personal property. Their knowledge serves to demonstrate and validate their sense of self-importance and to fulfill their personal ambitions.

Wishing to exploit their popularity, those who harbor such improper motives will further try to demonstrate their own significance by coveting a more prestigious name and position, a higher social status. They will behave as though no one can rival their success.

Swooning in the face of their own wealth and abundance of followers, these pretentious ones actually create causes for descent into the lower realms of existence. No longer a cause of liberation, their knowledge has actually become an obstacle.

People who have studied with worldly motives will boast of the long years spent acquiring and mastering their knowledge. When they encounter another person with a similar background, they will always find something to criticize. Meeting with someone who enjoys greater respect and reputation, they will be jealous and will search for defects and deficiencies in that person. Their knowledge becomes a recruiting tool to gather their own entourage, a means of amassing wealth and the trappings of mundane success.

Such people's knowledge will be a real obstacle for them, as well as serving as a hammer to bludgeon either those deemed inferior or those toward whom they are jealous. Isn't it clear that if we gather knowledge in the service of the mundane goals of this life, we are actually gathering the seeds of lower rebirth? Instead of thinking how our acquisition of knowledge can improve our worldly condition, we should focus our motivation and intent on the way in which whatever we study and learn may be useful to others. We must wish that our learning and knowledge will be something we can pass on to others in order to help them.

Another great benefit of knowledge, acquired through proper study that is pursued with sincere intentions, is that one becomes able to allay fears and anxieties in oneself and others. With proper motivation, the more knowledge one acquires, the more fear and insecurity one will be able to eliminate. The more fear you are able to dispel, the more you are able to increase the happiness of others as well as your own sense of well-being. Learning is not just a chore undertaken to acquire knowledge, it is in itself something enjoyable, something that brings satisfaction to oneself and can benefit others.

In short, if one acquires knowledge for the selfish goals of this life, it will lead to adopting a condescending attitude toward the unlearned and jealousy toward the more erudite. Study and the acquisition of knowledge will then serve to inflate the ego, which will simply increase our own suffering through binding us to worldly phenomena. Erroneous study, like artificial morality, engenders arrogance that may even lead to one becoming abusive toward others.

These are some of the ways that studying the Dharma can actually lead to lower rebirths, whereas study should serve as an antidote to save us from such a fate. What is the point of expending so much effort on something that not only does not mature us spiritually but actually increases our delusion? It would be better just to keep our time free to devote exclusively to mundane pursuits, interests, and goals! If we reflect and meditate well on the basis of these examples, it may become clear why Drakpa Gyaltsen urges us to give up all this foolishness. This song of experience by Drakpa Gyaltsen is a great teaching for practitioners of all different levels and speaks directly to those who are climbing the ladder of knowledge.

> All persons who practice meditation
> Are endowed with the antidote
> For abandoning the afflictive emotions,
> The root for accomplishing the path to liberation,
> And the seed for attaining buddhahood.

Having shown us the value, as well as some of the potential pitfalls, of the practice of ethics and study, Drakpa Gyaltsen's song moves on to the next topic, the practice of meditation. This is also relevant in the context we have been discussing, for if our practice of meditation comes out of attachment to this life, there can be unintended consequences.

Drakpa Gyaltsen first highlights how essential meditation practice is. Through the proper pursuit of meditation, the suffering and misery we encounter will be nullified. The motivation behind meditation must not be to seek solace in this life alone. It is only when our purpose is beyond the concerns of this life that meditation becomes truly significant. It is solely through the practice of meditation that all of one's efforts at study and contemplation will be brought to fruition. Every one of the great Buddhist masters achieved their high level of realization primarily through the practice of meditation.

This is why meditation is completely indispensable. Whatever intellectual knowledge we may have acquired, if we fail to gain experience and realization through meditation practice, then we will have no genuine realization to impart to others, even if we spend our days teaching. Gaining experience through the practice of meditation brings about a deepening of our confidence and faith, and leads in turn to genuine spiritual realization.

No matter how much we may rely on virtuous deeds and on study, these are still relative or conventional means to help us along the path. These conventional means are intended to foster realization in our minds. This means that we must begin to gain some realization of either relative or ultimate truth through pursuing them. However, to mature and fully ripen this realization, it is necessary to practice meditation.

By correctly following the process of meditation as prescribed by the tradition, we will not become stuck at the stage of mere intellectual knowledge. Rather, our knowledge will progress to become intuitive, derived from our own experience. Until we come to some deepening of realization that is based on our own experience gained through meditation, mere intellectual knowledge will be more of a burden than a liberating influence.

Whatever qualities of virtue and knowledge we may have previously acquired will be elevated and matured through the proper practice of meditation. Meditation is what enables us to sift through and refine our knowledge so that it can be of practical benefit to ourselves and others. Mere intellectual knowledge is not able to benefit ourselves or others and may even create obstacles to liberation. Meditation, on the other hand, leads to the realization of ultimate truth.

Meditation supports and enables us to become more flexible in our attitudes and perceptions and to apply the appropriate antidotes to negativities that arise. The more we are able to meditate, the more transparent our own problems and difficulties will become. Our troubles become easily manageable once our minds are sharp and clear enough to see how confusion has arisen in the first place. This enhanced clarity that comes about through meditative realization can prevent difficult situations from getting worse and can ensure that our patterns do not repeat themselves.

We need to come to appreciate the role and function of meditation on the spiritual path, and we need to embrace it with sincere motivation. It is by doing so that we plant the seeds of buddhahood in our mindstreams. Whether we are lay practitioners or have taken vows of ordination, whether we simply wish to eliminate everyday emotional problems or are seeking ultimate enlightenment, meditation gives a clarity and direction to our lives that we would not otherwise discover in the course of our normal experience. This is why Drakpa Gyaltsen encourages everyone to pursue meditation, and to do so with the right motivation.

Those who wish to learn meditation should seek out a qualified teacher and receive instruction. They should receive meditation teachings with the intention of directly purifying their own inner defilements rather than for any mundane purposes. Having done this, it is necessary to clarify and resolve any questions or doubts they may have regarding the meditation instructions. Then they will want to go to a quiet place and properly follow the guidelines, the techniques of meditation they have learned, using the methods as a means of directly remedying their own afflictive emotions. In order to apply the teachings to themselves, meditators need first to identify their own defilements or flaws and then to counteract these with the corresponding antidotes.

What are some examples of applying antidotes to negative attitudes by means of the practice of meditation? A beginner in meditation practice who suffers from attachment may meditate on repulsive-looking objects and the law of impermanence, reflecting on how everything will change and will not remain as it is. In this way, attachment is transformed into non-attachment. A beginner who discovers hatred in the mind may meditate on loving kindness and try to practice tolerance, patience, and compassion.

If one has ignorance, one may begin by applying analytical meditation in regard to the five aggregates or psychophysical constituents, to the sense organs and their objects, and so on, meditating on how these are related to one another. One proceeds in this way with analytical meditation on the law of dependent origination, as expressed in the Abhidharma teachings. This process does not remain confined to meditation sessions. At all times one's mind is constantly analyzing and examining what value there is in pursuing various objects and objectives. As a result of careful analysis, the meditator will be able to distinguish between what is beneficial and what is harmful. These teachings awaken the mind, provoking our interest in subtle details and processes, and thereby become an antidote to ignorance.

Thus, meditation teaches techniques through which anyone can remedy all types of afflictions and defilements. At first these will be reduced, and then eventually they will be eliminated. The elimination of the gross defilements and their latent impressions will enable the meditator to progress on to higher realizations, attaining the state of an *arhat*, a *sravaka*, or a *pratyekabuddha*. Finally, even the most subtle of the defilements, the obscurations to omniscience, are removed, and one attains *samyaksambuddha*, the state of ultimate enlightenment.

Meditation is the most effective remedy for whatever afflicts us, and it is through meditation that we are able to uproot suffering once and for all. We train ourselves to function in the state of meditation throughout the course of everyday life. Whether in a meditation session or in the post-meditation period, we are constantly mindful and know what to do and what to avoid.

We can begin to understand that the role of meditation stretches far beyond merely being an antidote to the suffering and difficulties of life. This is because meditation is the root cause of attaining liberation, *moksha*, a state totally free from the cycle of existence. Meditation is the crucial factor that enables us to reach ultimate enlightenment, buddhahood. Attainment of buddhahood depends on the authenticity of our meditation. All of the great masters have depended principally on the practice of meditation for their realizations. Progression on the stages of enlightenment known as the paths and spiritual levels (*bhumis*) is solely determined by the practice of meditation, never by intellectualizing. The stages of enlightenment, from the level of the *sravakas*, or hearers, all the way up to buddhahood, can only be perfected through one's own efforts in sustaining the practice of genuine meditation. Whatever spiritual qualities a person may possess depend on the strength of his or her meditation practice.

What we must understand is that regardless of how much we may study, regardless of how much we may train in moral discipline, if we do not endeavor in meditation, we will not attain enlightenment. There is no way we can even gain liberation, which leads to ultimate enlightenment, without meditation. There is certainly no way we can attain ultimate enlightenment without meditation. Truth, the nature of reality "as it is," can only be realized through the practice of meditation. When Buddha Shakyamuni meditated for so many years on the banks of the river Naranjana, leading to his attainment of enlightenment, he said that his realization came about through profound meditation.

It is possible that in the beginning meditation might seem tedious or tiresome. Later, after you acquire some experience and familiarity, you will begin to appreciate that the negative attitudes and perceptions we normally carry with us can be transformed through the practice of meditation. Those who have practiced meditation have developed some experience of their own, and it is the strength of this experience that enables them to further transform and reverse the negative attitudes and perceptions that arise in relation to all manner of situations. We apply what we have learned from our experience of meditation in our everyday lives.

The power of mindfulness we gain through meditation enables us to apply the appropriate remedy to any negativity that may arise. With mindfulness, when anger and aversion arise, we will discover that we are actually able to give rise to an attitude of loving kindness and compassion. In this way, as we become equipped with a repertoire of guidelines and instructions through which to train ourselves, meditation practice gives us the ability to directly eliminate negative attitudes and perceptions.

The type of meditation we are speaking of requires two qualities: "mindfulness" (*dranpa*) and "watchful noticing" (*shezhin*). There is a story from the *Bodhicharyavatara* of Shantideva that illustrates one sense of memory, remembering, and mindfulness (*dranpa*). While checking his storeroom, a man is bitten by a rat. He notices that he has been bitten, but nothing more comes of it. Then, after a few months, in the rainy season, the place where the rat bit him becomes swollen. He suddenly remembers, thinking, "Oh, maybe that was a poisonous rat that bit me that day." Noticing the swelling illustrates what is meant by watchfulness (*shezhin*), and remembering being bitten illustrates what is meant by mindfulness.

Maintaining mindfulness is extremely important. One important function of mindfulness is to enable us to remember clearly the instructions transmitted to us by our teachers. We must remember and be mindful of all the teachings and precepts we have received and taken; this is a key aspect of our practice of mindfulness (*dranpa*).

One important function of watchfulness, or "noticing," is taking note of whether what we are doing is right or wrong. Only through careful observation is a practitioner able to discriminate between what is beneficial and what is harmful, between what conforms to the ten virtuous deeds and what belongs to the ten non-virtues. Whatever the teacher has taught us must be tested, checked, and verified through our own experience. This is watchfulness (shezhin).

Meditation practice not only enables us to remedy the defilements that haunt our minds; it also imparts intelligence and wisdom to our daily activities. Wherever we are, whatever we may do, the strength of mindfulness and watchful alertness that we have developed through meditation creates a beneficial habitual tendency for us. This habituation to mindfulness and watchful noticing gained through meditation is what allows us to transcend all other contrary, conflicting habitual patterns.

Jetsun Drakpa Gyaltsen wishes us to understand for ourselves that there are two possible approaches to meditation, the superficial and the genuine. Although meditation is absolutely indispensable, it is said that one who meditates while seeking benefits, honor, and rewards for this life alone will experience a lot of contradictions and may suffer unfortunate consequences.

In regard to meditation, through your discipline of mindfulness and alert watchfulness, you will be able to observe whether your practice is in accordance with the genuine Dharma or with the worldly dharmas. You will be able to see whether or not you are motivated by attachments. Through self-observation and introspection, you can observe whether your intention and motivation for adopting discipline, study, and meditation have been corrupted or not. If they have, by guiding and directing your mind through mindfulness and watchfulness, you can find ways to adjust, correct, and improve your motivation and practice. Without mindfulness and attentiveness, we do not know how to distinguish between genuine and superficial practice. With mindfulness and attentiveness, we can make it our priority to practice sincerely and to shun any self-seeking pretense of practice.

Mindfulness and watchfulness awaken intelligence (prajña). With this foundation, we develop the intelligence that is, among other things, able to eliminate the negative side effects we may have accumulated through artificial practice. The development of intelligence gives our minds sufficient clarity to distinguish what is genuine about our practice and what is not. This intelligence is what reinvigorates our practice, giving us renewed energy and a freshened perspective. With this new perspective, we find ourselves able to perceive many qualities of the Dharma where before we saw only negativity.

Of course, while it is necessary to know how to make these important distinctions, this does not mean that from the outset our meditation practice will be completely authentic. It is most likely that those embarking on the path of meditation will notice that their worldly concerns are overly prevalent! Nonetheless, it is definitely true that as our motivation improves, mundane preoccupations will be minimized, and the qualities of meditation will be revealed and will flourish.

> Though there is no method [for gaining liberation]
> Without meditation,
> The meditator who practices for the sake of this life
> Is busy though living in seclusion:

In order to understand how the faults of artificial meditation practice may be exposed, let us again consider a variety of examples that may serve to guide our discernment. I'm sure many people will be amused and may find themselves laughing as they recognize some of these situations of which I will speak.

No doubt as an enthusiastic meditator you will try to go and seek out a quiet place, a place conducive to meditation. You will place your body there and close the door firmly so that no one and no thing can come or go. You might even bind your head tightly with a heavy blanket and squeeze your eyes closed in case anything jumps out to distract you. Still, somehow, your mind will sneak away, ending up in town or somewhere else it is not supposed to go. Many meditators, faced with this situation, use the time in solitude to catch up on their sewing work or other equally important tasks that they just could not find time to complete until now.

This is what will be likely to happen for those who meditate out of concern for the temporary improvement of their conditions in this life alone. It is said that even though such people may physically plant themselves in a place of great solitude, still their minds may be set loose into even more distraction than ever before. They may discover a greater throng of discursive thoughts than they ever knew they had.

If we meditate while our minds are mixed with worldly dharmas, or phenomena, then although our bodies may sit quite nicely, we are not in genuine meditation. We will be unable even to keep our minds inside the walls of our room, let alone stay with the focus of meditation. The eyes might be closed, but the mind is brightly lit by all manner of random discursive thoughts. However, one main function of genuine meditation is to tame the mind to the point where it can maintain a stable focus of meditation on any object for any length of time.

If you meditate while motivated by worldly aims, your mind will do more than just continue to wander about, running here and there whenever you find yourself alone. The minute you again meet other people, you may suddenly discover that you have so much to say, so many things to share, that you are desperate to catch up on anything you might have missed while you were "meditating." You will rush into irrelevant conversations with great zeal, just to make up for the deprivation you have suffered through remaining in isolation. You will roam about, in search of conversation.

When you are alone, you will find yourself planning your future dialogues. You will ponder well and choose with great care just those words that give weight to your realization and express its profundity. You will plan methodically how best to entertain and enlighten others with the fruits of your isolation. If you find yourself acting like this, you can be sure that you have remained consistently without any sort of stable mental focus. Regardless of what you may be doing physically, your mind has become more agitated, with more stress and tension than you had before.

Another interesting effect of remaining in isolation with questionable motives is that you will suddenly come up with all sorts of mundane things to do that you never had time to take care of before. You will see the retreat situation as the perfect chance to tie up all those loose ends. But this is not really what is meant by good meditation. In the same way, if we are entertaining thoughts about the news of the world, our mind is distracted, and this will cause our meditation to falter. We will have no remedy for this distraction, since we have not really bothered to learn what to do about these kinds of problems. Our faith will waver because of all the time we have wasted criticizing others rather than learning the teachings well.

> Reciting prayers by blindly chanting words,
> Ridiculing those who hear and contemplate,
> Jealous of others who meditate,
> And distracted in his own meditation;
> Cast aside this meditation of the eight worldly concerns.

If we seek the benefits of meditation mainly to satisfy this life's ambitions, then instead of being able to center ourselves, our thoughts may run wild. However many prayers and mantras we may say, our mind will remain preoccupied with the affairs of this life. Our recitation practice will have little more value than idle gossip, and we will not receive any of the benefits of recitation. In fact, we will fail to gain any realizations at all. Drakpa Gyaltsen is telling us that it is better to just give up this type of meditation than to deceive ourselves that something fruitful is occurring. He has spelled this out rather clearly, hasn't he?

Drakpa Gyaltsen's view is shared by another master, Dzapa Tulku, who observes the same kinds of situations. He says that even if one places oneself in a meditation room, closing the door tightly and claiming to be in retreat, then although the eyes may be closed, the mind may be set loose. This same teacher says that the mind may actually become more innovative in devising distractions than ever before. It may concoct all sorts of plans and schemes. The person may read, write, or get involved in any number of interests, which seem suddenly to blossom overnight, rather than actually persevere in the practice of meditation. Thus, it happens that whatever one chants in the name of meditative recitation may be disrupted by ordinary discursive mental chatter. Dzapa Tulku says that somehow this happens to him as well!

Drakpa Gyaltsen now provides us with other examples that can alert us to the fact that we may be approaching meditation with adulterated motives. One of these is that meditators who are afflicted by worldly attachment will criticize others who do not meditate as a way of praising their own practice of meditation or retreat. These practitioners will also tend to denigrate study as mere intellectualism and, in general, will always look for faults in others who may not be as diligent as they consider themselves to be. They will cast aspersions on the pursuits of scholars, asking how they could obtain any results since they do not make effort in the practice of meditation. Though such a practitioner may physically remain in retreat, yet the quality of their practice will definitely suffer the faults of distraction and dullness.

This is very important, since the quality of our meditation should not suffer from mental distraction. However much we may engage in recitation, this must be practiced with the appropriate degree of concentration, with the quality of sustained attention. If such focus is lacking, the practice will not be effective. To practice genuine meditation, we must master our own minds and engage in meditation with one-pointed resolve. In fact, whether we practice hearing, contemplation, or meditation, we must engage in these without entertaining any distractions. This is the key point. Then our practice will be very good. If we are practicing meditation with the more far-reaching goals of liberation and the benefit of others in mind, this motivation will produce the genuine sort of meditation that is free of distraction.

No matter how important meditation may be, for one afflicted with attachment to his or her own welfare in this life, meditation will end up becoming a cause for slandering others. Such a person may say of others, for example, "Their form of meditation is not right. They don't have the transmission, their lineage may be broken..." and so on. Again, the same person may be heard to remark, "There is nothing greater than meditation. Why are those people spending years and years studying? What a waste of time." In this way, a person may undermine the validity of the practices of others.

While such individuals may act like this, at the same time their own meditation practice is very distracted. The moment such people try to meditate, all they notice is how scattered their minds are, how impossible it is for them to develop any steady concentration and presence. Such practitioners will not only fail to obtain any lasting results from their practice, but they will continue to doubt the practices of others rather than questioning the authenticity of their own. They may say, "Oh, that person spends a lot of time in meditation. What a shame that he lacks comprehensive instructions and so is doomed to fail." This attitude is really nothing more than criticizing other meditators out of jealousy.

Such meditators may stay in retreat and yet find that they do not keep to the practice schedule around which their retreat is structured. They may find themselves consistently failing to start their practice sessions on time. Yet when they hear of someone who is following the requirements correctly, they will boast that they have done the same practice and may even claim to have finished the practice commitments more quickly than the other person!

In truth, when such practitioners are in retreat, their minds are not. They fail to tame their minds and are unable to achieve any of the signs and qualities that should arise from proper meditation. During rare moments of clarity, after they have made many efforts and have come to realize just how distracted they are, they may fall prey to doubt or self-loathing. They may think that there must be something wrong with them and experience fear or paranoia about themselves and everything else. They might even think that there must be something wrong with the instructions they received. As the saying goes, "The unskilled artisan blames his tools."

These are just a few examples that should make it clear that whatever efforts we make to retire into seclusion and exert ourselves in the practice of meditation will be fruitless if we act with the wrong motivation and intent. Drakpa Gyaltsen says that if we find ourselves in this situation, it is better to stop our practice for the time being. What Drakpa Gyaltsen is saying is that it is better to rely exclusively on worldly means to accomplish worldly aims rather than using spiritual means to pursue mundane ends.

To summarize what Drakpa Gyaltsen has shown us in regard to meditation, we can see that those who are afflicted by attachment to their present existence may practice meditation, but they will also criticize the meditation of diligent practitioners of whom they are jealous while looking down on others who do not meditate. At the same time, their own practice will suffer from persistent distraction and perpetual delusion. In this way is meditation afflicted by the eight worldly concerns.

If you wish to become free from attachment to mundane existence, it is necessary to meditate properly and to understand and abandon inauthentic and flawed approaches. Then meditation can truly become the root cause for alleviating the sufferings of this life as well as leading us through the stages of enlightenment. For this to occur, we must be able to distinguish between artificial meditation and genuine meditation that brings about realization. It is better not to meditate at all than to practice meditation in pursuit of worldly motives.

> What has been written up to this point is in accordance with the *Abhidharmakosha*, where it states, "Through possessing hearing and contemplation based upon moral conduct, one should thoroughly apply oneself to meditation." Thus, this shows directly the distinction between ultimate and relative aims, whereas it indicates indirectly the manner of meditating upon the difficulty of obtaining the [eighteen] prerequisites [of human rebirth] and upon the impermanence of life.

If it should happen that we find our own practice of meditation troubled by exactly the kind of faults we have been discussing, we may be greatly benefited by the practices of training the mind (*lojong*). In terms of what we have covered thus far, this means to reflect in particular on the teachings regarding precious human rebirth and the law of impermanence. We should train our mind, thinking, "Why should I waste the valuable time I have set aside for meditation by meditating improperly with misguided intentions? If I do not rectify these faults now, while I have the opportunity of a precious human rebirth, when will I again have the chance to redress and amend my practice?" We will gain a renewed sense of conviction and encouragement by reflecting on this precious human birth.

Otherwise, we may embark on the path of meditation only to discover at some later point that our intentions have been amiss. As a result, we may become discouraged and disillusioned and may even wish to abandon meditation altogether and never return to it. Therefore, it is very important not to become discouraged if we discover these faults in our practice of meditation, but instead to inspire ourselves through reflecting on the preciousness of human rebirth and the law of impermanence. This will help us to restore courage and confidence.

All of these teachings we have been discussing on the importance of adopting the proper approach to ethical discipline, study, and meditation also highlight, and require some understanding of, the difficulty of gaining a precious human rebirth. It is necessary to deliberately consider this well, which includes reflecting on moral discipline as the central contributing cause of gaining a precious human rebirth. It further requires that we contemplate the analogies and the numerical examples given in the sutras to illustrate the rarity of obtaining a precious human rebirth endowed with all the requisite qualities.

Pondering the rarity and value of this precious human birth will cause us to appreciate the opportunity we have and, consequently, will arouse in us greater diligence. Understanding that death is inevitable, we will be able to generate great enthusiasm for genuine ethical discipline, contemplation, and meditation, so that our life will not be wasted on fruitless pursuits and practices. Contemplating well the difficulty of obtaining a precious human rebirth, together with meditating on the nature of impermanence, will foster a great zeal for practice in us, infusing our practice with a quality of deep sincerity. This attitude will in turn engender tremendous progress on the path of Dharma.

Never take the privilege of this life for granted. Meditate on the law of impermanence and death so that you can truly avail yourself of this precious opportunity; then you will not inadvertently go astray. Precious human life offers a unique chance to gain liberation not afforded by other types of rebirth. These teachings ought to convince you that even having gained a precious human rebirth, a human birth in which one encounters the holy Dharma, many will squander it on superficial forms of practice that can only bear bitter fruit. Contemplate these points in order to arouse the motivation that you will not engage in Dharma practices out of concern for the goals of this life alone.

Precious human rebirth, a human life in which one meets with the Dharma and the requisite conditions, is extremely difficult to come by without having created the necessary store of positive karma in previous lifetimes. A human rebirth, while difficult to gain, is also impermanent. All that is born dies. All that meets will be separated. All that is accumulated will be exhausted. Since this is true, training the mind to understand impermanence will remedy exactly the sorts of faults we have been discussing.

To succeed in meditation practice, it is necessary not to delay the pursuit of meditation, not to procrastinate in any way. This life is perishable, it is fragile, and it may collapse at any moment. You can train yourself, thinking, "Since everything is impermanent and transient, so is my precious human life. While I have this temporary opportunity, I will practice diligently without procrastinating or making excuses." In this way a special enthusiasm, virtually impossible to acquire from outside of oneself, can be generated. This comes about through reflecting on these topics, and on the necessity of clarifying one's motives for practicing meditation.

A theme that has recurred throughout our discussion so far is the problem of jealousy as it arises in the minds of practitioners. If we are jealous of our Dharma brothers and sisters, this is very detrimental to our practice. Jealousy breeds disharmony in Dharma groups and may cause Vajrayana practitioners to damage the sacred commitments (*samayas*). There are some points you may keep in mind that may help in this regard.

It is best if close Dharma friends openly share their knowledge and experience, without any competitiveness. As long as they are following the same lineages of practice, this works quite well. On the other hand, if they are part of the same community but following different traditions, there is a possibility that disagreements might arise over whose way to follow. As for the question of sharing one's knowledge among fellow practitioners of one's own lineages, if, instead of guiding Dharma friends out of the goodness of one's heart, one attempts to direct others with the attitude that "I know better than you and you don't know anything," this sort of pride may well foster jealousy in others and make them indignant.

It is also important to rejoice in our Dharma friends and in whatever teachings they have received. The proper approach is that we ourselves should try to receive all the instructions from our masters and apply them to ourselves through our own practice and training. If what you receive makes you self-righteous and critical of others who may not have received as much, this again is completely inappropriate. This kind of pride may create jealousy among Dharma friends.

It is far better to rejoice in whatever virtue and Dharma activity your friends engage in, and to feel inspired to follow their example and do the same. In this way, Dharma friends help one another to improve. There is no need to be critical of each other. Critically comparing ourselves to each other creates jealousy and ill will. The real meaning of Dharma is to have a good mind, a good heart, and to have exalted motives and noble intentions. With this attitude, if one has knowledge or skills in Dharma practice and if one's Dharma friends may lack these, then with a good and generous heart one may guide one's friends along the path.

With this approach, everything should go well. As the teachings say, your path depends on your mind. When your mind is clear, the path is clear; if your mind is dark, your path will be the same. When your motives are in accord with the teachings and you are doing your best, then even should others doubt or misunderstand you, it is of no consequence. Everything is clear from your side. These are some ways we may avoid giving rise to jealousy in ourselves and in others.

What we have discussed up to this point essentializes the meanings contained in the quote from the *Abhidharmakosha*, mentioned in Sakya Pandita's annotations to Drakpa Gyaltsen's song, which speaks of the importance of ethical conduct, study, and meditation. In the *Abhidharmakosha*, Vasubandhu says that one should properly engage in meditation once one has prepared oneself through ethical conduct and has contemplated the relevant topics of the Dharma teachings. This trinity of factors, those of conduct, study, and meditation, should go hand in hand with one another. Our practice should not involve just one or two of these aspects.

No matter how many hundreds of great masters a person may have studied under, no matter how long one may have studied, if one's practice of morality, hearing, contemplation, and meditation is afflicted with selfish concerns for this life, one has simply earned a wealth of arrogance. Worldly attachments turn our Dharma activities into merely another form of materialism. Rather than leading to ultimate enlightenment, such attachments are the cause of lower rebirths and lead to ruin. A teacher corrupted by worldly motives will cause wrong views and a loss of faith to arise in the minds of disciples who may follow them. Please keep this in mind.

Thus far we have commented on Drakpa Gyaltsen's explanation of the first of Manjushri's four lines, "If you are attached to this life, you are not a person of Dharma." The general Buddhist teachings referred to in this first line are the teachings on the difficulty of obtaining a precious human birth as well as those on realizing the truth of impermanence and death. We will not go into all the details of these two now, as you may have already heard teachings on these subjects.

It is the tradition of our lineage that when teachings of this nature are imparted, this is not merely left as a teaching but is followed by reflective meditation in which we review the topics discussed. When we received this teaching from the great master Dampa Rinpoche, Zhenpen Nyingpo, the students would go over the teachings and practice meditation based on them, either individually or in groups. This is done in order to plant the teachings in our being as seeds of meditative realization. We should deeply feel the teachings at the time of hearing them, reflect on them during the breaktimes, and then try to gain some realization of them in our sessions of meditation.

3. Attachment to Samsara

(2)   If you are attached to cyclic existence,
                              you do not have renunciation.

In order to attain nirvana,
Abandon attachment to the three realms.
In order to abandon attachment to the three realms,
Keep in mind the faults of worldly existence.

HAVING SHOWN THE NECESSITY of reflecting on the precious human rebirth and the law of impermanence through his comments on Manjushri's first line, now Drakpa Gyaltsen's song turns to the contemplation of the pervasiveness of suffering and the shortcomings of conditioned existence. To contemplate the predominance of suffering throughout the lives of sentient beings fills the mind with weariness and sadness. It leads us to acknowledge the urgency of pursuing spiritual practice sincerely and with renewed enthusiasm, knowing how rare and precious an opportunity we now possess. At the same time it brings forth in us a sense of sympathy and heartfelt pity for all those beings less fortunate than ourselves.

Renunciation means that it is necessary to renounce the creation of causes that inevitably result in suffering. Worldly existence, samsara, is a bottomless pit of suffering. Those who cannot abandon or renounce suffering and its causes will never be able to reach nirvana. The word "nirvana" implies a condition that is free from sorrow. To reach this state beyond sorrow, to sever the root of birth and death, it is necessary to depart from the place of sorrow, which is worldly existence. In order to reach the state beyond sorrow, nirvana, a state untroubled by any form of suffering, it is essential to give up clinging to any of the worldly realms of existence. Attachment to this worldly existence will not lead one away from suffering and its causes, since all sufferings are only found in the context of worldly existence!

In commenting on the first instruction spoken by Manjushri, we considered the question of attachment to this lifetime and the faults that come from this attachment. However, the question of attachment goes deeper. It is not just a matter of giving up attachment to this life's rewards but of losing our taste and affinity for the whole of worldly existence. This is why it is necessary to contemplate and meditate upon the faults of conditioned existence. Otherwise, we may imagine that samsara possesses any manner of attractive qualities. Pondering the shortcomings of samsara should bring forth in us a tangible sense of disgust, as we are confronted with our own misguided pursuit of worldly ends.

To attain enlightenment, one cannot be attached to the three realms of existence, known as the desire realm, the form realm, and the formless realm. The desire realm is made up of the six or seven realms that are the abodes of the six types of beings of our universe, to which may be added a seventh class of beings, those in the *bardo*, or intermediate state. The form realm is composed of the seventeen levels of divine existence. The formless realm refers to the abodes of the final four classes of supreme formless gods. Sometimes the teachings speak of worldly existence in three alternate categories, that is, in terms of the "three existences": this refers to celestial existence, terrestrial or planetary existence, and subterranean or chthonic existence.

From among the three realms of existence known as the desire, form, and formless realms, the six realms of the six types of beings are subrealms within the first of the three realms of existence, the desire realm.

The form and formless realms are both celestial realms. In the celestial abodes of the realm of form, one has exquisite conditions and can enjoy everything with almost no struggle at all. Hearing this, one might feel attracted toward birth as a long-lived god. However, beings born thus are still enmeshed in worldly existence, and the nature of worldly existence is suffering. If one wishes to be born in those realms, it shows a lack of understanding of the real nature of samsara.

Being attracted to any form of existence, to any sort of personal status, power, or circumstances reveals that one has attachment to worldly life. Disenchanted with your own status, it is possible to harbor wishes to be someone or something else with a different position and with other conditions, not realizing that you would ultimately be no better off.

Drakpa Gyaltsen instructs us in the importance of developing a real sense of detachment in relation to worldly existence. If we do not understand that this existence is fundamentally flawed, it is easy to be attached to it. It is said that the basic underlying condition of every single type of worldly existence is that each of them is unsatisfactory; each is permeated with suffering. People may say that they are Dharma practitioners without really having renounced samsara at all. In order to be able to renounce cyclic existence, we have to give up or sacrifice our attachment to it.

If we are always pursuing a name for ourselves, chasing after special titles, wealth, a high position, status, and so forth, these are signs that we are still clinging to samsaric existence. If we say we have renounced samsara but still have small things we are unable to renounce, this means that we have not yet renounced. To renounce samsara, we must be able to sacrifice everything.

There are many traditional examples that show us how to regard worldly existence. If you visit a particularly unpleasant place, you will not wish to return there again under any circumstances. If you have this type of attitude toward samsara, it is a sign of renunciation. Another example of an appropriate attitude toward samsara is that of birds of the varieties that are unable to land on water; they would never even consider landing there. This is exactly how we should renounce samsara, so that we are determined that there is no way we are going to land there, no matter what; we know that we would drown immediately.

Also, consider a person who has a sickness that causes vomiting. As soon as he sees something revolting, he will immediately retch uncontrollably. This is how you should feel toward conditioned existence, a sense of revulsion rather than attraction. Another example that is quite appropriate is that if someone showed you a pile of excrement, you would not be suddenly attracted to go pick it up and play with it! If we are to develop renunciation with this sense of revulsion for worldly existence, first we need to know for ourselves the nature of dwelling in worldly states of existence. In our present state, we cannot possibly fathom the levels and degrees of suffering that are found throughout the conditioned universe. It is unimaginable.

What, then, are the shortcomings of worldly existence? In essence, there are three general types of suffering: the suffering of suffering, the suffering of change, and the suffering of all conditional phenomena. Every variety of suffering that it is possible to experience can be understood in terms of these three categories; all possible sufferings are subsumed within them. If we carefully consider the nature of worldly existence, we can find that it is completely ruined by these three kinds of suffering.

> First, the suffering of suffering
> Is the suffering of the three lower realms.
> If this is contemplated well, one's flesh will tremble.
> If it befalls one, there is no way one could bear it.

> Those who do not accomplish the virtue of abandoning it
> Are cultivators of the lower realms.
> Wherever they reside, they are pitiful.

To briefly look at the first of these categories, the suffering of suffering, it mainly concerns the suffering of the three lower realms, those of the hells, the realm of spirits or "hungry ghosts," and the animal realm. Those born in the hell realms must endure unbearable heat and cold. Beings born in the spirit world of the "hungry ghosts" are always tormented by hunger and thirst. Those born as animals suffer from their own dull stupidity, from being subservient or even tortured, and from living in fear due to perpetual uncertainty, insecurity, and so on.

The karmic plight of beings in the three lower realms is a great tragedy, because no matter what they do, no matter what they may try, their efforts only propel them into more and more woeful experiences. If we are born in the lower realms, there is neither method nor means available to us to remedy our plight. Beings of the lower realms are driven to act desperately in hopes of alleviating their suffering, yet all they are able to experience is more of the same.

The suffering of those born in the lower realms is interminable, without respite. There aren't any times when their suffering really abates, when they can breathe a sigh of relief and experience happiness. The suffering in the lower realms is so severe that there is no way one born under those circumstances can make any spiritual progress. We are indeed fortunate that we are not currently born in the three lower realms, since once trapped in such an existence, there are no means by which we may rescue ourselves. This is the suffering of suffering.

There is a text that addresses well the suffering of suffering, called *Traton Shulen, The Response to Traton.* Traton requested teachings from Drakpa Gyaltsen. In response, Drakpa Gyaltsen said that the suffering of suffering can be compared to the situation of a leper. People tormented by leprosy want to feel that they are going to get better. Whenever one of their leprosy boils comes to a head, they peel away the skin. This causes a powerful itching sensation. In response, they scratch and scratch until more skin comes off. They think that by scratching, they will feel better; yet the more they scratch, the more their disease is aggravated. We can reflect on this example in order to understand that no matter what beings born in the lower realms may try to do, it only increases their suffering, rather than lessening it.

Knowing this, then in relation to others, we should feel deep sadness for the unfortunate ones born in the lower realms. It is necessary to feel genuine pity for those miserable ones who have no way of helping themselves. At the same time, in relation to ourselves, we should give rise to a definite enthusiasm for the teachings, as well as a determination not to create causes that will propel us into such a sad states.

It is necessary to deeply meditate on these points again and again. Continue in this until you feel satisfied, until you feel that it is excellent that you are coming to understand the reality of these things and are developing conviction through your own experience. Meditate in this way and be grateful that you are able to strengthen your realization of the nature of samsara, that you are able to generate renunciation, and that you are giving rise to real pity for those trapped in lower rebirths. Continue meditating on these things with such intensity that your body shivers and goose bumps rise on your skin! This is how you should meditate on the suffering of suffering.

As you are meditating on the suffering of suffering, if you reach the point of shuddering in fear from merely thinking of these things, then you are ready for the next stage of the practice. For this, imagine what it would be like if you were compelled to endure an entire lifetime of continuous suffering under such conditions. It would be unbearable. If you contemplate this well, out of this will come real determination to stop creating the causes of these kinds of experiences. Once you have meditated on these things to the point of being viscerally moved, if you still continue to behave shamefully and ignore what you have learned, won't that be a tragedy?

There may be people who are not ready to take these matters to heart, who may not believe in any realms other than those of the animals and humans. They may believe that above us there is only sky and that below us there is only earth, so where is heaven and where is hell? However nice this may sound, this skepticism that dismisses the reality of heaven and hell is simply the expression of ignorance. These doubts arise from adhering to inaccurate views of existence, which simply creates more causes of suffering. Rather than being dissuaded by idyllic worldviews that are untrue, it is far more valuable to look deeply into the fearsome nature of the three lower realms of existence.

If you truly envision what it would be like to exist in these realms, it will certainly cause you to shake in fright, to tremble in fear. It is almost impossible to begin to imagine what it would be like to have to endure such a life. However severe the suffering in those states may be, due to the weight of their karma those born in the lower realms are unable to die for as long as this karma persists. Their suffering is so overwhelming that there is no way under those circumstances that they can make any progress toward a better life. This is what we must ponder, again and again.

In order to practice these meditations effectively, we must learn the details of these lower realms and the nature of the suffering experienced by the beings who are born there. The beings of the hell realms known as the cold hells experience continuous suffering. They are forced to endure unbearable cold, freezing for thousands of years. In the hot hells, beings spend the same periods of time in pits of burning fire, but they do not die.

The spirits of the hungry ghost realms must bear relentless wrenching hunger and parching thirst for thousands of years without the slightest sustenance. Due to the heaviness of their karma, they are unable to die prematurely but suffer continuously until they have exhausted their karma for being born there.

Regarding the spirit realm, the realm of the hungry ghosts, although there are a great many varieties of these beings, there are three main categories by which they may be known: those which are externally distorted, those which are internally distorted, and those under the power of the "distortion of distortion." None of these have any chance of finding any food, since nothing in their environment manifests as something edible. Even if they could find a bit of discarded mucus, as soon as they put it in their mouths it turns into flames and scorches all their internal organs.

As for the animals, they, too, are under the power of the suffering of suffering. Human beings will not hesitate to drain their milk from their bodies. We will plunder them for their hair, adorn ourselves with their skins, and devour their flesh without the slightest consideration for their welfare. Animals are constantly attacked by one another. They view each other as walking food. If right now we were forced to undergo a day in a typical animal's life, there is no way we could possibly bear it or wish to remain there.

Since at this time we have no memory of our own direct experience of the three lower realms, it is necessary to meditate deeply on being born in those realms. One vividly imagines oneself there in one of the lower existences, for as long as one is able to, until this arouses an immense sense of sadness and hopelessness. There was a great master, Langtangpa, who was known as the "dark-faced one" because he never smiled, overwhelmed as he was by the knowledge of the intensity of the suffering of suffering. He wept continuously because not only could he see the suffering of beings, but he could feel it for himself. Through this kind of vivid entry into the suffering of the lower realms, imagining ourselves born in those conditions, we will be able to gain some experience of the suffering of suffering and develop real empathy for the ill-fated ones who find themselves in these realms.

The possibility that we could be there in actuality, physically experiencing such a life, should indeed cause our flesh to tremble in apprehension and fear. To come face to face with this as a genuine possibility can send shockwaves of fear right through us the moment we realize that there is no way we would be able to endure such torments if we were suddenly to find ourselves in the midst of them. If we can give rise to these waves of shock and horror, this is very valuable to the practice of Dharma, as it will engender in us a powerful sense of renunciation. If you truly contemplate the sufferings of worldly existence, there is no time for anything other than tears. Right now we cannot bear even a pinprick or a spark of fire, but the suffering of the lower realms is incessant. It is the suffering of suffering, sufferings heaped one upon another, suffering multiplied by suffering.

Once we have entered into the suffering of the lower realms to the point of being able to feel it for ourselves, we must understand the causes and conditions that produce these tormented states. This will lead in turn to our abandoning all such causes and conditions. When you have seen the causes and conditions that have led beings to the lower realms and have empathized with the suffering of those realms, then you can truly renounce them. Knowing the reasons that beings experience such torments, do your best not to be attached to worldly existence. In order to be able to renounce samsara sincerely, you need this inner experience of the nature of the lower realms.

How can we turn away from the causes that lead to birth in these realms? Since birth in the hells is the direct result of anger, then whenever you are in danger of giving rise to anger, remember vividly and immediately that this is a cause that will propel you into rebirth in the hell realms. When stingy and miserly reactions arise in you, remember well that indulging these emotions creates causes that propel you into existence as a hungry ghost. When dullness, doubt, and confusion muddle your mind, remember that this produces causes that drive you toward rebirth among the animals. In this way you practice a very important aspect of remembering and mindfulness (*dranpa*).

If we have really pondered and meditated upon the nature of worldly existence, how is it that we can still continue to heap upon ourselves causes that will lead to exactly such experiences? If we fear the sufferings of the animals, the realm of spirits, and the hell realms, why are we not planting the seeds of fortunate existences and instead cultivating a path to these inferior births? Is it not pitiful, this unconscious oblivion in which beings continue to imprison themselves? If you carefully contemplate such extremes of suffering found within the three lower realms, it can engender a profound sense of urgency, causing you to strive to create not the slightest karma that would lead to such a rebirth. When these facts are understood, there is no way that you can refuse to act on them and continue on as you have in the past.

Drakpa Gyaltsen asks us why are we not seriously finding ways to restrain ourselves from non-virtuous deeds, which are the direct causes propelling us down into the three lower realms, instead of actually cultivating the very causes that will take us there? In our world, those who commit very negative deeds usually end up in prisons. Most beings, without knowing it, are accumulating those very causes that will, in their next birth, imprison them in the lower realms. Were it not so tragic, one could almost laugh in disbelief at how beings could be so foolish. This is a cause for great sorrow.

This is why it is necessary that we not only hear about, know about, and begin to acknowledge these realms but that we contemplate and meditate on them in order to actually give rise to a powerful sense of renunciation. This renunciation needs to be so great that one feels a deep revulsion toward any actions that would lead to such painful experiences. We must at any cost learn to restrain ourselves from the deeds that lead to this primary type of suffering, known as the suffering of suffering.

> When contemplating the suffering of change, one sees:
> The movement [of beings] from heavenly realms
> To the lower realms;
> Shakra reborn as an ordinary being;
> The sun and moon going dark;
> And the universal emperor reborn as a slave.

Next let us look at the second category of suffering, the suffering of change. While the suffering of suffering includes all the sorrows of the lower realms, the suffering of change applies to the beings experiencing the higher realms of samsaric existence. Drakpa Gyaltsen says that if we wish to consider the meaning of the suffering of change, we can start by simply observing the transitory nature of all beings. Though we are all gathered here today, one day not one of us will remain. We will have parted and gone our own ways, and this meeting may seem never to have taken place.

There are countless examples of beings taking birth in the higher realms and then, nevertheless, falling into the lower realms. This is true even for the creator god Brahma, and for Shakra or Indra, the lord of the gods who rules over our physical world. They may indulge their good fortunes as if these will endure forever, but actually they will end up being enslaved by different beings of lowly birth just as soon as their positive karma has been exhausted.

Consider those gods who are born as the spirits of the sun and moon. They are like princes of our local universe, having the power to illuminate the darkness of the world. In the Buddhist context, the sun and moon are not regarded as planets but as sons of the gods who inhabit huge masses of land, their celestial palaces radiating light like the rays of the sun. Yet in the future, it is inevitable that they will be born in a place so dark that they will not even be able to see their own outstretched hand, themselves unable to shed even as much light as a firefly.

The definite results of the suffering of change are completely inevitable. Even the most powerful universal monarchs, who have exercised supreme power over the entire universe, will in later births be enslaved and imprisoned. They will be forced to work as porters or beg for their food, utterly unable to recapture their former estate. It is the same with kings, prime ministers, and presidents — all authorities. They may hold great power one day and be helpless the next.

Beings in the higher realms have no guarantee that they will remain in that exalted state, since all is subject to change. However long their pleasures may last, they won't last forever, and when they are over, conditions usually reverse themselves and the opposite is experienced. Those who have been attached to their prior fortunes suffer accordingly. There is no definite certainty that accompanies favorable circumstances, from the state of the highest world ruler down to the common pleasant conditions that ordinary beings enjoy. All these conditions are transient; they fade away. As soon as they are gained, they begin to slip through our fingers. This is the suffering of change.

Although beings may gain higher rebirth, if they fail to continue to carry out skillful virtuous deeds in the course of their lives, they will deplete all of their accumulated virtue, even as they are enjoying the ephemeral happiness of their present conditions. When the residue of positive karma is exhausted, then having failed to skillfully accumulate uplifting deeds, they will be forced to experience their own downfall.

> Belief in this depends upon the word [of the Buddha],
> As ordinary people do not have the ability to realize it,
> So observe for yourself the changes of men:
> The wealthy become poor, the mighty become weak,
> Where there were many people there is [only] one, and so on,
> Exceeding the imagination.

Even though a person may have faith in these teachings concerning the law of impermanence and the transitory nature of all things because they come from the sutras and the teachings of the Buddha, ordinary people are generally not ready or even able to fathom the deep implications of the transient nature of existence. Although Buddha himself has thoroughly explained these matters, we still have not been able to comprehend them.

Drakpa Gyaltsen says that if you have difficulty gaining realization of the changing nature of things, take some time to observe how the human condition is always changing. Look at the examples of those you may personally have known of, people who were so rich and then became so poor. There are those who perhaps had everything, and suddenly circumstances changed and they became destitute and penniless, not even owning as much as a needle and some thread.

In the same way, consider those you may have known about who were very powerful and prestigious, only to become weak and impotent, ignored by their former admirers. Reflect on known cases of those who have wielded great influence, only to become irrelevant. Likewise, contemplate situations where very close friends have become foes who cannot get along. These are common experiences of the suffering of change with which we have all come in contact.

Observe for yourself situations where once there were many and now there are few, large families that have simply died off so that only one member has yet to disappear from this world. You may return to a place that you knew well only to find that no one you knew remains, that others have taken their place. Look at the condition of those once honored by many, who are now left unattended with no one to take notice of them. Before, everyone obeyed their orders. Later, no one pays them any mind. There are endless indications of the suffering of change occurring all around you if you wish to see them; it is impossible to list them all. For this reason it is good to personalize things, to reflect on your own life. Look within and remember all the changes you have gone through. Consider this in terms of health and fitness, relationships, fortunes and misfortunes, and so on.

All of these topics for reflection have been classical examples, taken from the scriptures, of the suffering of change as it afflicts all beings in general and one's own human existence in particular. From this enquiry we can see that there is no certainty whatsoever in the human condition and that there are no circumstances that are sure to remain pleasant so that we ought to aspire to experience them. For as soon as we have them, they may vanish. There is nothing that is permanent, and therefore, nothing can stay the same, no conditions can endure. Thus, all of us must experience the suffering of change.

There really is no end to the examples of the changing nature of all things. There is not a single sentient being who is unaffected by the transitory nature of all phenomena. Whatever pleasant conditions we may acquire, they will only last for a while; nothing remains for very long. When we come once again to experience unsatisfactory circumstances, this is the suffering of change.

The teaching of impermanence is a great support for practitioners. In the early stages of practice, the truth of impermanence will encourage you to enter the path. In the middle stages, it will impel and drive you to practice well. Bringing to mind what we have realized through meditating on impermanence will remind us to practice with great diligence. Otherwise, we may forget what we are supposed to be doing! Finally, in the end, impermanence will help you to realize the true nature of mind.

Though we have gathered here together, one day none of us will remain. We will have parted and gone our own ways, and our meeting will seem never to have taken place. Due to this fact, we need to meditate on the changing nature of all things and, through this, to let go of attraction to any of the states of existence to which we might otherwise become attached. What is most important is that as soon as you encounter any transition to more favorable circumstances, it is necessary not to become caught up in the situation. Instead, it is better to learn to let go of attachment to such circumstantial, ephemeral happiness immediately, from the very beginning, as soon as it arises. This is the key point. This is how to approach the suffering of change.

> When contemplating the suffering
> Of the nature of all conditional phenomena, one sees:
> No end to activities,
> That suffering exists among many and among few,
> And that suffering exists among the rich and the poor.

While we have contemplated the suffering of suffering and the suffering of change, what primarily afflicts human beings is the third type of suffering, the suffering of all conditioned things, the suffering of all conditional phenomena. Even if one is somehow able to cope with the suffering of change, one still cannot escape the suffering of all conditional phenomena.

What does this mean? First, Drakpa Gyaltsen says that however much we may have done and accomplished, we are never able to say that we have finished all of our work and activities. This is the ceaseless, worrisome sense that there is still something that we must do, some reason that we must keep constantly busy. Without ever actually increasing the satisfaction derived from our activities, we feel certain that we cannot stop. Everything is conditional, but not understanding this, we become the victims of our own endless agenda. Regardless of whether we gain any real contentment from our actions, we fall victim to the neverending busy-ness of trivial pursuits. This is one important aspect of the suffering of all conditional phenomena.

To begin to understand this, it is necessary to reflect on the suffering involved when one always has something one must do, the suffering of a mind continuously occupied with a multitude of tasks. As human beings we know that there is never a period of time when we feel satisfied that our efforts have been adequate, when we feel that everything has been completed. Yet we lack the wisdom to simply stop. Are all these lists of things to do, concocted by our minds, ever really finished, however much attention we give to them? In the end, we are not finished until we simply stop. Things never seem to be done by doing; they only seem to be done when we stop doing!

Until we realize that it is impossible to gain more satisfaction by doing more things, at the very least we should not be compelled to do things simply for the sake of keeping ourselves busy. The very nature of our activities is that they are never completed no matter what we do. This is why it is said that nothing gets finished by doing something; it is only when you put it aside that it is finished! Since the ceaseless nature of worldly activities means that they never afford us any contentment in their pursuit, can we not find the courage to stop? Only one who is becoming free from the attachment to worldly existence will have the humility and courage to put a stop to everything.

The next point Drakpa Gyaltsen would have us consider is that whether there are many people in our life or only a few, neither case seems really satisfactory. When you have many people in your life, you have many "people problems" such as relationship conflicts and so on. When you have few people, there seems to be much that is missing, unfulfilled, and you lack the support to get things done.

It is the same with wealth. Whether you have great wealth or very little, it doesn't matter. If we do not have it, we crave it. If we have it, how will we manage to keep it? There aren't really any cases of people becoming genuinely happy simply due to becoming wealthy. The rich suffer just as much as the poor do. There are simply different problems lurking there as soon as one has wealth.

If you investigate this for yourself, you will find that it is not the case that being wealthy means being happy and that being poor means being unhappy. First, the wealthy create negative karma to acquire their fortunes, and then they must jealously guard their property. They feel they should hoard their possessions and may become stingy and miserly. They are filled with worry and suspicion of others' motives. In this way, wealth becomes a prison one cannot escape. The wealthy have property, animals, and servants, but their worries rise with their wealth. And yet, how can they put an end to their suffering, since the very status they covet is the cause of their unhappiness? Although they desire wealth, it does not bring them happiness, but instead compounds their suffering.

Likewise, neither are the poor happy or satisfied. They must constantly try to obtain something, hoping that something might come into their possession to alleviate the poverty they suffer. They may continuously covet the wealth of others, wishing and hoping that if they could only have this or that, they would be happier. They do not understand that happiness is not caused by wealth or the lack of it.

We fail to acknowledge these truths because the suffering of all conditional phenomena is so pervasive. No one is clever enough to outsmart these facts of existence, to become happy in spite of these inevitable conditions. This is the nature of all composite phenomena. Each of us has aggregates that compose our being and a consciousness that abides within them. These are always under the power of the universal nature of suffering.

> All of human life is exhausted in preparations,
> And everyone dies while making preparations.
> Those preparations do not end even at the time of death,
> [When we] begin preparations for the next life.

Since it is the nature of all conditional phenomena that there is no certainty, that there are no guarantees in the midst of such conditions, why bother with ceaseless trivial pursuits that bring neither satisfaction nor realization of any kind? Whether we spend our time acquiring wealth and possessions, pursuing education, or whatever, no matter how many years we may spend in such pursuits, our preparations are never truly completed. Today we must prepare for tomorrow; next week we must prepare for the following one. Aren't we really spending our time preparing simply in order to prepare some more? From this perspective, doesn't our whole life stray into exactly these sorts of preparations, only to end up ultimately being wasted? Our whole lifetime is spent in activities that are finally left unfulfilled. It is in this sense that these activities are futile.

An ordinary lifetime is so utterly consumed planning and preparing for this and that, yet even as we approach the moment of death, we haven't really finished our tasks. We are simply at the beginning of a new task—dying! All these endless plans only lead us, at the time of death, to the point of having to start another lifetime, where we will once again be caught up in the perpetual busy-ness that has never brought us any sustainable satisfaction in any of our previous lifetimes.

What good does it do us to gain yet another lifetime if the life we have just spent has not brought real gratification, in spite of all we have done? Even when we finally die, the ending of this life is also just another preparatory activity—preparing for our next life! Even dying doesn't finish things, since when our next life comes, we will once again have countless things to accomplish that we will once again never be finished with. Therefore, Drakpa Gyaltsen speaks of the necessity of being able to restrain ourselves, to abandon and relinquish all our activities, all of our racing here and there without actually getting any-where. Why can't we pause for a moment and truly reconsider whether or not these activities are really meaningful?

What Drakpa Gyaltsen has been showing us through all of these illustrations is the importance of developing renunciation. A crucial element of what we must renounce is our attachment to doing things. If we ourselves do not put a stop to our activities, they will never cease on their own. Once we are able to be free of attachment, we reach the state beyond sorrow. Without becoming free of attachment, this will never occur.

> Those who are attached to this world of existence,
> Which is a heap of suffering, are pitiful.

It is said that those who understand how ephemeral and hollow of meaning their activities actually are also understand that all these activ-ities are also the means by which we voluntarily heap more suffering upon ourselves. It is very sad, pitiful, that beings do not realize this. Rather, they arouse all the efforts of their body, speech, and mind toward doing just those things that amount to nothing.

All beings who are born as a result of composite factors, such as the aggregates that make up a human being, are subject to this most sub-tle of the three types of suffering, the suffering of all conditional phe-nomena. The suffering of all conditional phenomena is subtler and hence more difficult to understand and overcome than the other two types of suffering. This type of suffering is not so easily detected, and there is no definite remedy for it, no methods that can allay it. Without coming to some realization of ultimate truth, the suffering of all conditional phenomena is very difficult to remedy.

There is nothing about worldly existence that is certain or reliable. Death is certain, but we fail to contemplate it and instead barely think about it. All the while, we continue to cultivate the causes that lead to further unreliable, unstable circumstances. One has no certainty in regard to how long one will live; when one dies, one has no certainty where one will be reborn. There is no guarantee we will not be born in the three lower types of rebirth, unless we properly follow the Dharma teachings. If we do not follow the teachings properly, there is every likelihood that we will be reborn there, since we are busy creating the causes of these births all the time, day by day.

Up to this point, the faults of the world of existence have been directly shown, whereas what actions should be taken up and [what should be] rejected have been indirectly indicated in accordance with the law of cause and result.

The second line of Manjushri, and Drakpa Gyaltsen's commentary on it, explicitly describe the shortcomings of samsara, and implicitly demonstrate the teachings on the law of karma, cause and result. Any experience of suffering we undergo is linked to non-virtuous deeds we have enacted elsewhere. It is necessary to reverse our karmic pattern of accumulating negative deeds. We do this by increasing our store of positive actions and thereby neutralizing and transforming our repository of negative actions.

Be confident in the law of cause and result. Whatever you do, your good deeds will be excellent causes of happiness. Since your wrongful actions create the causes of unhappiness, then that is what you will experience. It is necessary that we learn to discern this relationship between causes and their inevitable results. Through this we learn to restrain ourselves from the cultivation of negative causes and in turn to create fortunate causes through wholesome deeds.

Until you can effectively change the pattern of your actions, words, and thoughts by acquiring insight into this teaching of the law of cause and effect, you will not gain much genuine realization of the shortcomings of samsara. This is a key point. The only way you can gain this kind of realization is to understand what must be adopted and what must be abandoned or renounced.

All of these contemplations are meant to lead us to the knowledge that the nature of worldly existence is unsatisfactory. All realms of existence, from the highest realm of the gods down to the lowest of the hell realms, partake of one or two, if not all three, of the general types of suffering. We need to sincerely reflect and meditate on the nature of these three types of suffering, using the examples that have been given, in order to develop a steadfast sense of renunciation.

If one learns to abandon attachment and clinging to worldly existence and its endless activities, one will be able to go beyond the sorrowful and woeful nature of the world. If one has no attachment to worldly activities, to this life, or even to this existence, it becomes possible to pass beyond sorrow to nirvana, where all inner foes have been destroyed. To go beyond sorrow means to be free of afflictive emotions, the inner enemies that lie hidden in our being. Letting go of attachment, clinging, and fixation enables us to reach at last a state beyond suffering.

If we understand the futility of activities, all of which bring no ultimate happiness, then we also learn to restrain ourselves from deeds that bring only suffering. A person who learns how to refrain from actions that cause suffering therefore also learns to adhere to the infallible law of cause and result, the law of karma.

4. Attachment to Selfish Purposes

(3)   If you are attached to your own purpose,
                you do not have bodhichitta.

When free from attachment, nirvana is won.
When nirvana is attained, bliss is obtained.
This song of experience is the
Parting from the Four Attachments.

Liberating myself alone is without benefit,
Since all the sentient beings of the three realms are my parents.
To leave my parents in the midst of suffering
While desiring my own bliss is pitiful.

JETSUN DRAKPA GYALTSEN tells us that he wishes to further narrate his song of experience on Parting from the Four Attachments. In explaining the meaning of this third line spoken to Sachen by Manjushri, Drakpa Gyaltsen says that in order to attain nirvana, it is necessary to develop non-attachment. This means that one must genuinely part or separate oneself from the kinds of attachments we have been discussing. In order to help us to understand how to attain nirvana, he says he is compelled to give further spontaneous expression to his meditative realization.

The teachings we have contemplated thus far should generate in us a sense of the urgent necessity of renouncing worldly existence and seeking liberation from samsara. Drakpa Gyaltsen says that if one is able to renounce samsara, one will attain nirvana, bliss, and happiness. But now he asks us, what is the benefit of gaining the bliss of nirvana for oneself alone?

Drakpa Gyaltsen questions us, voicing his realization that it would do no good at all for ourselves alone to attain liberation, would it? What would there be to gain from being the first to reach the "finish line" of enlightenment? If the world is full of suffering, he asks, What is the benefit of myself alone attaining enlightenment? We would be leaving behind all sentient beings in the three realms of existence, who at one time or another have been our own kind mother and father. To simply ignore their plight now would be deplorable. Would it not be a cause for shame for us to reach a state of enlightenment while abandoning all sentient beings, who have been our own mothers, in the dense forest of suffering? Those who seek liberation for themselves alone should indeed be pitied.

Drakpa Gyaltsen encourages those of us who have reached this stage to now reconsider our intention to renounce worldly existence in order to find lasting happiness for ourselves alone. He informs us that we must now examine more deeply the motivation with which we have sought liberation, until we come to feel saddened or even ashamed at the thought of exclusively seeking our own liberation.

It has been declared by Shantideva in his *Bodhicharyavatara* that the childish strive after their own benefit while the enlightened devote their efforts toward the welfare of others. The noble ones who follow the path of selfless altruism will come to experience the freedom of enlightenment. On the other hand, the immature endlessly worry about themselves, remaining mired in worldly existence. If we wish to understand the difference in the results of the demerit created by selfishness and the merit acquired through altruism, this is well illustrated by comparing a childish sentient being with a fully enlightened one.

All the unwelcome suffering we must endure originates in selfishness, without a doubt. Just look at all the sentient beings who have been single-mindedly chasing after their own welfare, almost without interruption, yet have never derived any lasting happiness. In contrast, a fully enlightened being, who has pursued the benefit of others, has achieved the bliss of the exalted state of buddhahood.

All the suffering of the lower realms, whatever difficulty and unhappiness we may experience as human beings, as well as every other possible suffering of the three realms of existence, have their origin in cherishing ourselves more than others. Even if we obtain a precious

human rebirth again in the future, we will encounter the same difficulties of sickness and misfortune, all the same hardships. These have
their origin in our mind having fallen prey to ignorance, attachment,
and aversion. We feel attached to those we regard as loved ones and
aversion toward those we dislike, and we are generally ignorant regarding those toward whom we are indifferent. These attitudes create
unwanted suffering.

It is further explained in the teachings that whatever happiness we
experience, whether it be short-lived or enduring, has its origin in
kindheartedness and altruism. If we work for our own ends and purposes, we inevitably encounter suffering; if we work for the benefit of
others, we meet with happiness. When pursuing our own welfare,
without fail we become completely ensnared in the three defilements,
the three mental poisons of ignorance, attachment, and aversion, do
we not? This is why running after our own welfare creates suffering.

Even practicing the Dharma, if done for our own benefit alone, will
not lead to complete liberation. There is nothing final to be gained
through seeking liberation for ourselves alone. This teaching on the
third line of Manjushri extols the virtues of altruism and demonstrates
that we do not ultimately benefit from pursuing personal rewards.
Rather, the noble ones teach the necessity of dedicating ourselves to
others. This has been taught well by Shantideva in the *Bodhicharyavatara*, and is found in many other teachings as well. We have habitually become so accustomed to thinking of our own benefit, yet we have
never truly succeeded in this endeavor. Would it not be better now to
consider the matter differently?

For this reason the bodhisattvas have put forward the idea of radically changing our priorities. Rather than making our own welfare the
highest priority, they have suggested putting the welfare of other living beings above our own and making this our foremost concern. If all
suffering originates from a selfish motivation and if our selfish motivation has failed to bring us happiness but instead has led only to suffering, what harm is there in heeding the advice of the bodhisattvas and
trying the opposite?

Hence, Drakpa Gyaltsen goes on to reveal the importance of cultivating altruism, which is the intention to benefit sentient beings, as a
far more elevated reason to practice Dharma than the mere pursuit of

our own liberation. In fact, to gain our own liberation alone should be the least of our priorities. Drakpa Gyaltsen is showing us how one is able to benefit others as well as oneself through altruistic intentions, by generating bodhichitta, the wish to attain enlightenment for the sake of others. This is the most valuable of all endeavors, and we should definitely pursue it from this point onward.

These views sung by Jetsun Drakpa Gyaltsen have been thoroughly expressed in the written works of the Indian master Chandragomin. Chandragomin says that when he thinks of gaining personal liberation, he feels so ashamed that were he to continue to harbor such thoughts, he would never wish to look upon his own face again! Even to think of seeking his personal liberation while leaving his own kind mothers behind seems so shameful to him that he vows never to think such a thing again. Rather, he resolves to radically shift his motivation, his whole basis for seeking liberation

Thus the third line spoken by Manjushri to Sachen Kunga Nyingpo is devoted to the development of altruism, the precious bodhichitta, or "mind of enlightenment." Bodhichitta is the intention to free other beings from suffering and establish them in the state of enlightenment. While we enter the Buddhist path through taking refuge in the Three Jewels, we are also taught that it is necessary, as a result of taking refuge, to give rise to a good heart, to a compassionate mind that seeks the welfare of others. Chandragomin is telling us that instead of running after personal liberation, we ought to reevaluate our motives. He recommends that we do this through remembering the kindness of our own mother.

If we want to understand what it really means to seek our own liberation while abandoning other sentient beings, this is illustrated by a very clear example. It is said to be like the situation of a person who enjoys great wealth while his mother has become a destitute beggar. Shouldn't someone like this feel utterly ashamed of himself for his lack of gratitude and for refusing to repay his mother's kindness, in spite of possessing ample means to do so?

Following this example, any practitioner who recognizes the importance of developing altruistic intentions toward others ought to feel the same pangs of conscience at the thought of abandoning sentient beings. Reflecting deeply on this example should then cause them to decide firmly not to pursue a selfish course. No matter how long it may take them, they will resolve not to seek their own liberation but will instead aspire to remain in samsara until all beings are liberated. They will dedicate all the virtue they are able to accumulate toward the welfare and happiness of all sentient beings.

Once we have determined to reach this noble state of mind, we must follow a tradition of contemplation and meditation. In the beginning we need to first arouse the strong wish to bring happiness and the causes of happiness to other beings. This is known as the practice of loving kindness. To generate the precious bodhichitta, the intention to attain enlightenment for the sake of others, it is necessary to first cultivate loving kindness toward other living beings. This begins by meditating on our own mother, reflecting on how indebted to her we are. We need to contemplate all of the kindness our mother has shown us, from the day we were conceived right up to the present. She has consistently devoted the fruits of her labors so that we might be raised and educated.

When we follow this line of contemplation, we are able to recover an amazing store of memories recounting our mother's acts of kindness. We see for ourselves how concerned she was for us, how she held our best interests in her heart. If we do this contemplation well, these things we recall will completely transform the way we remember our mother and will completely recast the relationship we have with her. Our relationship with her will become much healthier and more affectionate, and we will truly wish her to be happy and have all the causes of happiness.

A variation on this same practice is to meditate on the love a mother has for her only child. With either of these meditations, we first develop some real feeling and then gradually expand this feeling until it includes all sentient beings. An interesting effect of performing these contemplations well is that we will be much less obsessed with ourselves as a result. When the welfare of our mother becomes a heartfelt priority and we are genuinely concerned with what we can do to further her happiness, directly or indirectly, we are definitely cultivating loving kindness.

When we wish our mother to be well and happy, we naturally also wish that the happiness we are able to provide her should not be subject to impermanence, to the suffering of change. This wish leads us to develop compassion. Our mother's suffering, or even potential suffering, becomes our own. Put yourself in her place, feeling her troubles and whatever hardships she has to endure. Through this you develop such sensitivity and empathy that you become able to feel her pain as your own. This kind of feeling will cause you to make every deliberate attempt to reduce the suffering of your mother and to prevent any likelihood of this suffering returning. This is the practice of compassion.

Through contemplation and training in the wish for our mother to be well and happy and to be free from suffering and the causes of suffering, we cultivate the twin practices of loving kindness and compassion. The result and culmination of these two practices can then become the altruistic motivation of bodhichitta, the thought of enlightenment. An altruistic motivation arises through wishing that others have happiness and the causes of happiness and that they be free from suffering and its causes. The union of the two qualities of love and compassion, which comes about through the force and power of these two wishes, is what is meant by the altruistic motivation.

Once a heartfelt altruism is generated in ourselves as a result of these contemplations, this creates an amazing sense of affection and closeness toward our mother. Once we have given rise to this feeling, we are able to extend it to others. Gradually, as our meditation continues to progress, we will be able to expand the feeling of love, gratitude, and compassion until it comes to embrace all living beings. This expansion of our love and compassion is possible because in the past, since time without beginning, every being has in fact been our own kind mother. As is said in many refuge prayers, "For all sentient beings who have been my mother, I take refuge."

This is the way in which we are genuinely able to give birth to bodhichitta, the thought of enlightenment. Once bodhichitta is awakened, this profound intention gives us an amazing patience we have never before possessed; it gives us strength and courage we never before knew. Once we have developed the deeply felt resolve to separate all sentient beings from their suffering and its causes, this means that the practice of compassion has definitely taken root in us.

Shunning the disgraceful attitude that abandons sentient beings, we should accept the grace of repaying the kindness of others, giving rise to altruism. This leads to the awakening of bodhichitta, the thought of enlightenment. To have bodhichitta, the wish to free others from suffering and establish them in the state of perfect enlightenment, not only means that we always wish for the welfare of others, it also means that we will always sacrifice our own welfare for the sake of others. If we want to have bodhichitta, we should take to heart the words we speak and recite as practitioners. We may say, "I am acting for the sake of all sentient beings," while our behavior may not correspond in any way to that statement. If the words we speak are not supported by our actions and conduct, then we do not have the genuinely altruistic bodhichitta attitude.

This is why we begin by generating a great strength of aspiration and then learn to follow this up with actions. These two, which are known as the bodhichitta of aspiration or "wishing" and the bodhichitta of application or "doing," together constitute what is known as relative bodhichitta. Bodhichitta is of two types, relative bodhichitta and ultimate, or absolute, bodhichitta. Ultimate bodhichitta will be the topic under discussion when we come to the fourth line spoken by Manjushri.

Relative bodhichitta is concerned with how we initially train the mind. This must be done so thoroughly that we become habituated to altruistic thinking, and it becomes the natural tendency of our mind. This tendency gains momentum until we dedicate whatever virtuous conduct we engage in, however small, so that all sentient beings may attain buddhahood. This is the bodhichitta of aspiration, the "wishing" thought of enlightenment. Understood more deeply, bodhichitta really means to have a vast mind, an intention so inclusive that it embraces all beings.

Having pondered and taken these things to heart, one is really able to dedicate whatever one does for the benefit of other beings. Right now we are more accustomed to adopting a selfish attitude. For this reason, we are taught to offer prayers that we may be able to turn our backs on selfishness and turn instead to cherishing the welfare of others. An important aspect of this is the dedication of merit, as we are dedicating the benefits of whatever good we have done for the sake of all beings. Sending forth for the benefit of others whatever virtue we accumulate is part of the practice of exchanging oneself for others, the next step in the authentic cultivation of bodhichitta.

In the first lines of the *Madyamakavatara* of the Indian Buddhist pandita Chandrakirti, it is explained that *arhats* and *pratyekabuddhas* of the lesser vehicle are born from the words of the Buddha, from the teachings. Chandrakirti says that there are three causes that produce a bodhisattva, a sublime being on the stages of enlightenment (*bhumis*) according to the greater vehicle: the first is compassion, the second is the wisdom that realizes the emptiness of the self and the emptiness of all phenomena, and the third is bodhichitta, both relative and ultimate. Finally, Chandrakirti says that a perfect buddha is born from a bodhisattva. These lines of Chandrakirti are brief, but their meaning is vast, and they have been commented on extensively by Chandrakirti himself and others. In the present context, his words make it clear that one cannot attain buddhahood without bodhichitta.

> Let the sufferings of the three realms of existence ripen
>   upon me,
> And let my merits be taken by sentient beings.
> By the blessings of this merit
> May all sentient beings attain buddhahood.

All sentient beings within the three realms of existence have at one time been our own kind mother and father. Just as you have direct parents during this lifetime, so all sentient beings have also been your own parents. We need to understand this well if we are to recognize our deep affinity with all beings. If we have understood this, it ought to be clear by now that it would be a mockery if we were to abandon all of these loved ones to the suffering of existence. If we are unable to have faith in these words of the Buddha, this is a real pity. Just because we are able to look after ourselves, what kind of accomplishment is that? Rather, we should try to find a way to rescue every being from the suffering of conditioned existence. For this we must first learn to regard other beings as more important than ourselves.

How does this come about? Once we have established a heartfelt altruistic motivation as a basis, we will be able to properly meditate on equanimity, on the equality of self and others. In addition to developing love and compassion, we also need to give rise to the immeasurable quality of equanimity. In this regard it is important to understand that every sentient being wishes to be happy, just as we do. They do not want suffering, just as we ourselves do not. Reflecting on this will enable us to empathize, to put ourselves in the other person's place, to meditate on the commonality and equality of ourselves and all other beings. This is the practice of equanimity, of equalizing self and others.

The meditation on this equality leads us to being able to actually exchange self for others, which means to exchange our own happiness for the suffering of others. By learning how to exchange your own happiness for the suffering of others, you begin to cultivate the genuine altruism known as bodhichitta, the mind of enlightenment. Bodhichitta must be authentically generated and aroused. It is most important that we should not feign kindness and compassion, merely to impress or influence others, while lacking within ourselves the real feeling that ought to accompany such acts.

The followers of the way of the bodhisattvas pray, "May all the sufferings of other living beings ripen upon me; may all my happiness reach other living beings." The great masters of the Kadam tradition were amazing practitioners who meditated on these teachings. In a famous account, one of these masters once saw someone throw a stone at a dog. This teacher, who had genuinely practiced exchanging self with others, actually fell off his throne, exclaiming as though he had been injured. When the stone struck the dog, the master shouted "Aro!" and fell off the throne! Most of those present thought he was just pretending. But in fact, the stone that had struck the dog in the ribs had bruised the master's ribs. This occurred because he was practicing so deeply the meditation of inviting the sufferings of others upon himself. Just as the master was able to transfer the pain of the dog to himself so that the dog would not have to experience it, so our mind training can enable us to forsake our own happiness and actually be able to alleviate the sufferings of others.

Sometimes people are afraid to undertake this training. They think they may become sick and unhappy if they invite all the suffering of others upon themselves. In fact, this is not the case. The more suffering you are able to feel and imagine that you absorb, the more you will increase your accumulation of merit and wisdom. Practitioners who are well trained in exchanging self and others can actually visualize and take upon themselves the suffering of others. Then the other person suffers no harm, nor is the practitioner harmed by taking on another's suffering. The bruise on the side of the master was only a sign of the practice, but the master was uninjured. Bodhisattvas are overjoyed to enact this kind of conduct, to actualize their aspirations in this way. This is the quality of real bodhisattvas.

This kind of power to help others is available to us, but we must train very well in order to be able to perform the exchange of self for others in actuality! However, just trying to gain this ability is already very beneficial. First you must have the wish and really feel it, and later you will be able to actualize it. In order to understand the suffering of others, we must empathize with them, we must feel what they are feeling. There is a famous bodhisattva in the sutras named Thar Thung, who had such love and compassion for beings that he was always weeping uncontrollably, stricken with the suffering of all sentient beings. Through empathizing with others in this way, we are also able to understand their wish to be free from suffering.

In order to be able to abandon any particular experience of suffering, we must know the cause of that experience. The cause is negative deeds, the ten non-virtuous deeds of body, speech, and mind. This is why the Buddha taught that his whole Dharma is concerned with cause and effect, or karma. As an ordinary person learning to follow the way of the bodhisattvas, when we see another being suffering, we first learn to feel and empathize with them; we may even be able to see some of the causes for their suffering. Then we make wishes and aspirations that we will be able to liberate them from their suffering and from the causes of their suffering. These prayers and aspirations have power; through our prayers alone, those who are afflicted can certainly be helped. This is what we can do for other beings in our present condition.

As we have said, this training begins with the meditations on the equality of self and others, with equalizing self with others. It begins as we come to the realization that all others wish happiness just as we do and that all others wish to be free from suffering just as we do. This part of the training is not so difficult. The practice of exchanging self for others may be a bit more challenging.

We should first train to follow this practice by meditating upon it according to the instructions. One day we will actually be able to take on the sufferings of others, just as the Kadam master in the story was able to do for the stricken dog. It is difficult to meditate in this way. Who wants to actually exchange their happiness for the suffering of others? Yet if you familiarize yourself with the principles of this practice and give it a try a number of times, you can begin to see its merits. Seeing for yourself the benefits of such a noble attitude, you will naturally be persuaded to adopt it as a way of being.

The sublime intent of the bodhisattvas is summarized in the wish, "May all the sufferings of the beings in the three realms of existence ripen upon me; may all my virtue and happiness ripen upon other sentient beings." This is how practitioners of the way of the bodhisattvas should learn to give away their own happiness while inviting onto themselves the suffering of others.

This brings us to the meditation practice known as "sending and taking" (*tonglen*). In order to practice sending and taking, recite prayers and wishes such as those we have been discussing. Visualize that all of your happiness and virtue shines forth as bright rays of light that illuminate all living beings. Likewise, visualize that all the suffering and misery of all living beings is attracted toward you. Just as a razorblade shaves hair from the head, the sufferings of other living beings are cut away from them to ripen upon you.

As we mentioned, sometimes beginners in this practice are fearful of undertaking it, thinking that it will bring harm to them. There is no need to be fearful, the practice will definitely not harm you, but it will bring you great benefits. You will not really lose your happiness through the practice of exchanging self with others. In fact, your merit and also your realizations will increase. For this to occur, it is not enough to simply pray and visualize exchanging your virtue for the suffering of others. You need to feel it and mean it.

Once our mind has been thoroughly trained to the point where such selfless altruism becomes our everyday mentality, we reach the stage where it becomes possible to test whether or not we are able to actualize our intentions, to act upon our wishes. This is what is known as the bodhichitta of application, the bodhichitta of "doing." For this, we engage in the practice of the six transcendental perfections (*paramitas*), which together constitute the conduct of the bodhisattvas. This means that we engage in generous giving, discipline ourselves through ethical conduct, practice patience, cultivate enthusiastic diligence, train in concentration and in meditation, and develop wisdom. Whatever of the six perfections we enact, this becomes the proving ground of our aspirations and the means of actualizing our wishes.

When we begin to discover that our aspirations have been actualized, have actually come about, this will impart a deep and enduring satisfaction. This in turn replenishes and reinvigorates the strength of our altruistic intentions, which might otherwise fade over time if we never put them into practice. The actualization of our previous wishes revives our spirits and encourages us to continue to cultivate further altruistic intentions, directing these toward ever more beings.

Giving rise to the sincere intention to be of benefit to others and following through on this with deeds enables us to help others effectively while at the same time purifying negativities and accumulating merit. We have discussed how practicing the bodhichitta of aspiration, or "wishing," leads to training in the bodhichitta of application, or "doing."

Finally, to have authentic bodhichitta, our conduct must correspond to the words that fall so freely from our mouths. Wise persons with realization are able to sacrifice their own limbs for the sake of all mother sentient beings. Great beings, bodhisattvas, are really able to practice like this. However, we are well aware that we ourselves are not yet able to practice in this manner.

When we are happy and have all the favorable conditions present, we do practice somewhat. If we are lacking in any of these favorable conditions, we give up our Dharma practice. This is a sign of lacking the strength of bodhichitta, the true altruism that strives to attain enlightenment in order to free all beings from suffering. Once we begin any kind of practice, we must persevere, follow through with it all the way, until we reach the goal of the practice as it is described in the Dharma instructions.

Once we have trained ourselves through generating altruistic wishes and following these up with actions, we are ready to test our training further by entering even more deeply into the meditation of exchanging our own happiness for the suffering of others. This means that we want to be able actually to give away our own happiness and receive in turn the suffering of others. One prays, just as Drakpa Gyaltsen prays in his song, "May the suffering of all living beings, those who dwell in

Chogye Trichen Rinpoche.
Photograph by Thomas Kelly.

Great Maitreya image at Jamchen Lhakang in Boudhanath, Nepal.
Photograph by Mark Rose.

Manjushri.
Courtesy of Shelley and Donald Rubin. http://www.himalayanart.org

Jetsun Drakpa Gyaltsen.
Courtesy of the Rubin Foundation. http://www.himalayanart.org

Sachen Kunga Nyingpo

Courtesy of Shelley and Donald Rubin. http://www.himalayanart.org

Dampa Rinpoche Zhenpen Nyingpo.
Courtesy of David Jackson.

Nalendra Monastery.
Photograph by Chogye Trichen Rinpoche. Courtesy of David Jackson.

Zimog Rinpoche.
Courtesy of David Jackson.

Chogye Trichen Rinpoche.
Photograph by Raphaele Demandre.

the three realms of existence, ripen upon me. Whatever meritorious deeds I have accumulated, however great or small, may they all be shared and taken by other living beings."

Practitioners who have sincerely invoked this prayer and integrated it into their being may then courageously test themselves in meditation through the practice of sending and taking (*tonglen*). Here, you meditate upon the totality of your own happiness, and on all the causes of happiness to be found in your own life. Reflect on what gladdens you and brings you joy, on all the gifts and blessings in your life, to the point of really feeling joy and gratitude for what you have received. Feel and imagine this like the brightness of the sun's rays, shining from your heart and radiating forth as light rays that illuminate other beings. In this way, you meditate with the intention of actually transferring your happiness, virtue, and merit to other beings. This becomes the further cultivation of loving kindness in which you have been training your mind in the preceding meditations.

Once you have done this, visualize and imagine that you take upon yourself the sufferings of other beings. Imagine that all the suffering of other beings is cut away from them, in the way one would shave one's head with a sharp blade. All their suffering is cut away and swiftly drawn to you and absorbed into you. All that afflicts them is completely eliminated, and they are freed from suffering and its causes, just as you have wished and intended through your practice of compassion. This is the further cultivation of the practice of compassion that you have already developed in the earlier stages of meditation.

Meditating like this again and again on the practice of sending and taking (*tonglen*) is the process by which we develop the meditation of exchanging self with others. We train our minds to habitually function in line with the prayer of the bodhisattvas that the suffering of others ripen upon us and that our virtue be given to them. We dedicate the fruits of our practice with the wish that all living beings may attain the state of buddhahood swiftly and without impediment. To deepen our realization of the practice, it is not enough merely to pray and visualize this process. In this further stage of the training, we must generate an unshakeable resolve that now we will *really* take upon ourselves the suffering of others while transferring our merit to them.

Bodhichitta enables us to sacrifice our own welfare for that of others, to always cherish all mother sentient beings, to remain unconcerned about our own personal welfare. These are the qualities of a true bodhisattva. People may think or even say, "Oh, I am a bodhisattva." But if their conduct does not truly represent these qualities, if their behavior does not reflect the sublime character of the noble ones, then regardless of what they say, they certainly do not resemble bodhisattvas.

While practicing thus, the great exponents of altruism, those who follow the teachings and try to emulate the deeds of the bodhisattvas, have made prayers and aspirations in accord with these principles. Most essentially, they have prayed:

> May the sufferings of all living beings
> Of the three realms of existence ripen upon me.
> May the merit and virtue that I have earned
> Be taken from me and given to other sentient beings.

You must first of all generate this aspiration, making strong wishes and prayers, before you can become capable of actually bringing this about in practice. In order to be able to train yourself through these prayers, you must have the courage to change the quality of your heart, to be truly different, even to be able to recite such prayers. This is because you must be willing to accept your fate if your prayers actually come true! This is the measure of your practice.

Not only this, but you must aspire to gather an abundance of merit and happiness, vast enough to actually have something to give to all sentient beings. Then you can wish that all the meritorious deeds you have already accumulated may be taken away and enjoyed by all sentient beings. This aspiration must first be developed through training yourself in prayer. Then, later, if it actually happens that someone takes something of value from you, you will never experience any suffering as a result, since this is exactly what you have prayed for.

Once you have gained realization in the practice of exchanging self for others, you will even be able to be reborn intentionally in places where there is suffering. Once born there, you will also be able to alleviate the suffering of the beings there and lead them to liberation. You will not be born in such situations through the force of karma but through the force of your aspiration, and you will possess the capacity to help the beings you find there. The bodhisattva prays, "By the virtue of taking on the sufferings of beings and giving them my merit, may they be liberated." These aspirations have real power.

In this way, all of the bodhisattva precepts contained in elaborate detail in the Lamdre teachings of the Sakya school as well as in many other traditions are actually included in these two lines of aspiration. If we choose to commit ourselves to caring for the welfare of other living beings, less suffering and more happiness will definitely come our way. Therefore, Drakpa Gyaltsen concludes his verses on the meaning of Manjushri's third line by giving voice to the aspiration of the bodhisattvas:

> Let the sufferings of the three realms of existence ripen upon me,
> And let my merits be taken by sentient beings.
> By the blessings of this merit
> May all sentient beings attain buddhahood.

> *Up to this point, the meditations on loving kindness and*
> *compassion, which are the causes [for the production of the*
> *enlightenment thought], have been indirectly indicated, whereas*
> *exchanging self and others, which is the result [of the*
> *enlightenment thought], has been shown directly.*

In summary, Manjushri's third line is about abandoning the attachment to one's own purpose, since without doing so one cannot follow the practice of the bodhisattvas. Drakpa Gyaltsen's words regarding the third line of the teaching of Parting from the Four Attachments emphasize the importance of developing bodhichitta. In addition, they implicitly indicate how this is developed by the meditations of loving kindness and compassion, and they explicitly teach the importance of exchanging self for others. Finally, Drakpa Gyaltsen reminds us that it is necessary to dedicate all the virtue we accumulate for the sake of all other sentient beings, our own kind mothers.

If you live your daily life according to the priorities we have laid out here, you will find a state of happiness and contentment in which you value and appreciate whatever you have, however small it may be. This is because the power of these aspirations made by the bodhisattvas enables us to dedicate whatever we have to benefit all other living beings. However dreadful the sufferings of other living beings may be, one has the courage and determination to be able to take them upon oneself through this noble idea of the bodhisattvas.

When one truly has the motivation to liberate all sentient beings, only then is it possible to attain the result of the three bodies (*kayas*) of buddhahood, or complete enlightenment. With lesser motives, such as those of the Hinayana vehicle of personal liberation, one will receive a lesser result; one's level of realization will be far less exalted.

All that we have discussed so far in relation to the third line of Manjushri belongs to the training of relative bodhichitta. The training of ultimate bodhichitta will be discussed in great detail in the next section of our commentary, in relation to the fourth line spoken by Manjushri. In the present context, we can say that those who have not learned to recognize the true nature of mind, ultimate bodhichitta, are only able to exchange themselves for other beings and to try to eliminate the suffering of others through prayer, visualization, and empathizing with others. However, if one knows how to recognize the true nature of mind, and mixes or merges the exchange of self and others with the recognition of mind nature, this is the best possible way to practice this exchange. One who has some realization of the nature of mind can do this practice within the recognition of the view.

In the relative sense, the awakening of bodhichitta consists first of the motivation to attain enlightenment for the sake of all living beings and then of the application of this motivation through the practice of the transcendental perfections. The ultimate awakening of bodhichitta includes the realization that the true nature of all living beings is utterly free from all the varieties of temporary, conceptual confusion that normally deludes them. In fact, all beings share the true nature of phenomena (*dharmata*), which is emptiness. All beings have awareness-wisdom (*rigpai yeshe*), the luminous clear light of the nature of reality. The true nature of all living beings is the expanse of primordial purity (*kadag ying*). This essence is present in all living beings, and it never leaves them, but they fail to recognize it. Recognizing it is the ultimate awakening of bodhichitta.

Since all beings possess this nature, all living beings can be awakened to buddhahood. In reality there is nothing that really exists, since everything shares the nature of emptiness. This means that ultimately all sentient beings, by nature, do not really exist. Beings are deluded because they believe in the existence of something that is actually unreal, that is by nature empty. Acknowledging this within the recognition of the uncontrived nature of mind is the ultimate awakening of bodhichitta.

Knowing this, recognize awareness-wisdom in the emptiness of space. Rest freely in this uncontrived state, where the last thought has passed and the next thought has not yet arisen. This is the ultimate bodhichitta. The teachings on ultimate bodhichitta describe the real way, the ultimate way, to benefit other beings. If we can practice in this way, this is one of the greatest ways of practicing the Buddha's teachings.

5. Attachment in the View

(4)   If grasping arises,
                       you do not have the view.

In whatever manner I continue, there is no liberation
Through grasping at the true nature of things.
To explain this precisely:
There is no liberation through grasping at existence,
There are no heavenly realms through grasping at non-existence,
[And] grasping at both [extremes] is [only] done in ignorance.
Be joyful in the state of non-duality.

THIS BRINGS US to Manjushri's fourth line, "If grasping arises, you do not have the view." This last line is extremely important. In order to elucidate the meaning of this line, Jetsun Drakpa Gyaltsen goes on to say, in effect, "However I may consider myself, I should dwell in the nature of absolute reality (*dharmata*), just as it is in itself." The great Drakpa Gyaltsen has also said, "Whether I sit up or lie down and sleep, I remain continuously in the suchness of reality as it is (*dharmata*). I always remain in the nature of the mind, as it is."

Drakpa Gyaltsen is telling us that it is necessary to remain in the nature of the sphere of reality, the space of the true nature of phenomena (*dharmadhatu*), regardless of what activities we may engage in. Regardless of what we do or how we move about, our mind should not part from the bare, all-inclusive space of the nature of phenomena. We are speaking of realizing the nature of mind in its nakedness. Drakpa Gyaltsen's advice is never to stray from this awareness, never to grasp or fixate on anything.

The admonition that one's view must be free of grasping is crucial to the realization of emptiness. This realization includes the understanding of "non-arising," which begins with the knowledge that something does not arise from itself, nor does it arise from anything other than itself. Through progressive insight, one proceeds to establish the absence of any inherent or true "existence." Not even a tiny seed inherently exists by itself. All things only appear to exist according to conventions, based on the various causes and conditions that make them appear. Nothing is actually there on its own, and nothing exists in its own right, so there is nothing to cling to or fixate upon.

Why is it necessary to properly understand these things in order to realize the true nature of mind? Without the correct view, even if one perseveres on the path, one will still go astray. So first of all we must understand that if we mentally grasp on to any view or realization, there will be no liberation. This also means that if one becomes fixated on any viewpoint that stands in opposition to another, one will not be liberated.

For example, if one falls into the extreme positions known in the Buddhist tradition as eternalism and nihilism, one will not even be able to reach the levels of liberation attained by the *sravakas*, or hearers, and the *pratyekabuddhas*, or solitary awakened ones, of the Hinayana vehicle. When such grasping and fixation is present, non-attachment is impossible. If one abides in truth or reality (*dharmata*) just as it is in itself, one is already free from the duality or dichotomy of mentally grasping at "existing" and "not existing," free of clinging to notions of "it is" and "it isn't."

To explain this further, Jetsun Drakpa Gyaltsen says that those who expound the validity of existence, who insist that there is an eternal existence of things, are known as eternalists. They are obviously not able to attain a state of liberation, as they are unable to chart an alternative course for themselves, believing as they do that things already exist as they are, eternally. In fact, grasping at an eternal existence actually prevents us even from attaining rebirth in the higher realms of samsara.

If in your view you attach yourself to "existence," this is known in the Buddhist tradition as holding the position of eternalism. From this position, there is no way even to seek liberation. To attain liberation and enlightenment, we must realize emptiness, the true nature of all phenomena. Therefore, if you grasp at your own being as having a truly existing self, or if you fixate upon phenomena as having some truly existing identity, there is simply no way to gain liberation or enlightenment.

On the other hand, rather than taking the eternalist position, if you mentally grasp on to the opposite perspective, the aspect of emptiness alone as the view, you may stray into the other extreme position acknowledged by Buddhist philosophy, that of nihilism. Those who hold the view of nihilism deny the possibility of liberation and reject the inevitability of the law of cause and effect, thereby rejecting the possibility of future rebirths. Nihilists feel no inclination to create causes for higher rebirths, not to mention the causes for liberation. Nihilists believe that all things end in non-existence.

Those who hold nihilistic positions or viewpoints believe in a null-and-void final absence of anything. Adherents of such views are led to deny the merits of doing good deeds and to deny the negative karmic accumulations that result from bad deeds. One who follows such ideas finally ends up with a worldview that acknowledges no sins and no virtues. This is the worst and most dangerous sort of nihilism, as it completely repudiates the law of cause and effect, the law of karma. One who persists in such errors has not the slightest chance of gaining a higher rebirth in samsara as a human or a god, let alone of attaining liberation from samsara.

It is impossible for such persons to attain either higher birth or liberation because they are oblivious to the ripening of their deeds. They do not know that whatever they do will ripen upon them in the future. Due to this mistaken attitude, they will have no interest in accumulating the positive merit of virtuous karma since they fail to acknowledge any possible benefit of engaging in virtue. As we have thoroughly explained, without the practice of virtue it is impossible to be reborn in the higher realms of existence.

Thus, it is said:

> For those who hold to nihilism,
> there is no way to gain the higher realms.
> For those who hold to eternalism,
> there is no way to gain liberation.

Since grasping and fixation are the cause of suffering, it is first of all important to know how to avoid getting caught up in grasping at the two extremes of affirmation and negation, the assertions of "it is" and "it is not." You should contemplate it in this way: If one takes the eternalist position and grasps at some sort of real, eternal existence, there can be no liberation, no freedom from such an existence, can there? One is holding on to "something," but this "something" is not actually there! On the other hand, nihilists who deny a real existence and hold to the view of the non-existence of things cannot attain even a higher rebirth. Since they deny that any good results come from the practice of virtue, they have no reason to engage in it! As a result, their future suffering is inevitable.

In both of these cases, there is no "middle way" view possible. Once we have understood this, we must ask ourselves if there is an alternative to this basic dilemma. Since it is also impossible to adhere to both the eternalist view and the nihilist view at the same time, would it not be much better to abide in a state that renders the dichotomy of "existing" and "not-existing" irrelevant? Therefore, Drakpa Gyaltsen says, "Why shouldn't I dwell in a state of mind that is free from these two extreme positions?"

Drakpa Gyaltsen explains, "Since I do not wish to fall into either the extreme of eternalism or that of nihilism, and since I cannot hold both positions at the same time, I would rather remain in the non-dual state, the all-pervasive nature of the sphere of reality (*dharmadhatu*). Rather than clinging to the eternalist view and rejecting the nihilist view, I must free myself from grasping at either extreme position and remain without fixation in the natural state of my own mind."

Thus, Jetsun Drakpa Gyaltsen is directing us to the ultimate truth, to the way that we can recognize and sustain our recognition of the true nature of our own mind. For this, it is first necessary that we do not trouble ourselves with the notions of eternalists and nihilists. The predicament they present needs to be invalidated, nullified. Once you have resolved this dilemma for yourself, you are free to abide in equanimity, in the emptiness of all things. Drakpa Gyaltsen is suggesting that what we must do is come to rest in equanimity, in the nature of reality that is beyond expression and elaboration. Without making the slightest attempt to express what it "is" or what it "isn't," simply remain equally in the state of non-dual meditation.

If we truly take to heart the teaching on Parting from the Four Attachments and meditate on its meaning, this will be very profound and will benefit us greatly.

> *Up to this point, having rejected the views of eternalism and nihilism, the general method for placing the mind in the non-dual state [of the inseparable merging of subject and object, existence and non-existence, and so on] has been shown.*

All phenomena are mind's sphere of experience.
Do not seek a creator in the four elements,
In chance, in God, or the like,
But be joyful in the nature of mind itself.

Drakpa Gyaltsen has begun his song on Manjushri's fourth line with general statements on the nature of ultimate truth. However, this approach alone may not help the beginner to actually realize the true nature of mind. So Drakpa Gyaltsen proceeds to guide us step-by-step, beginning with the "Mind Only" or Chittamatra viewpoint of Buddhist philosophy. He says that everything experienced is created and projected by one's own mind. There is no component of our experience that does not hinge or depend on the mind itself.

Quoting these lines of Drakpa Gyaltsen, some Buddhist dialecticians have alleged that the Sakyapas are followers of the Chittamatra or Mind Only school of philosophy, also known as Yogachara or Vijñanavada. However, when one looks more deeply into what Drakpa Gyaltsen is saying, his view doesn't stop at the view of "mind only."

If we do not discover the true nature of mind, we may actively believe that things exist outside of our minds as some sort of objective reality, stemming for example from a divine authorship where an all-powerful "God" creates the "world." This leaves us at the whim and mercy of things that are outside or other than ourselves. Those who believe in this way are not and cannot be free, since they are convinced that whatever they experience is real or objective, created by something else. As we have discussed, if we say that our own experience is caused or authored by another, then we are always waiting for conditions outside of us to alter themselves in a way that is favorable to us. That is going to take a long time, for certain!

Those who cling to such views of "existence" believe that their understanding is correct. However, all the phenomena we experience are created neither by gods nor by supernatural beings. Neither is it true that phenomena are only material. The materialistic view is the scientific view, which holds that phenomena are based only on material elements. Those who hold this point of view say that only when material elements come together do things manifest. Or they may say that phenomena only exist when different material particles interact.

Materialists hold a view of existence that is based on the principle of "matter." They believe that whatever they perceive through the senses truly exists, that the material world is real, because it appears so real and tangible. But this viewpoint is also not accurate. To arrive at the true view of reality, one should avoid extremes such as belief in an externally created existence or in an exclusively material world. For those who hold these views of clinging to existence, there can be no liberation.

Furthermore, according to the Mind Only school of Buddhist teaching, while on the one hand it is true that this world is not created by any supreme being such as Ishvara, or by anyone else, on the other hand it is also true that everything is fabricated by one's own state of mind. All appearances are mind. Nothing exists outside of the mind's sphere of experience. Mind is the substratum that creates and projects all phenomena. As it is within, so it is without.

This is where the Buddha offers us an alternative to conventional viewpoints, stating that nothing is created by anything other than one's own mind afflicted by karma and defilements. The Buddha himself has made it clear and demonstrated at great length that there isn't any supreme being that creates anything at all. Hence, because the conventionally held beliefs are neither logical nor in fact true, what is the point in entertaining these inaccurate views of reality, imagining phenomena to be created by something other than one's mind?

Similarly, in regard to the materialist view, we need to ascertain that neither the physical world nor our subtle physical body is created from intrinsically existing elements. Whatever may appear to us is none other than our mind, manifesting the entire spectrum of forms we perceive. These forms are distorted appearances of the mind itself, which only seem to exist independently of, or external to, oneself. If all the phenomena we perceive are actually our own minds, then it must be our own thoughts that construct our experience.

Let us use a simple analogy. If we wish to designate a particular mountain as "a mountain in the east," this is only possible in reference to another place, called "the west." The mountain in the east is not in any inherently existing "east." The term "east" by which the mountain is designated is relative, referential. In the same way, all dualities, such as right and left, short and long, up and down, only make sense to us in reference or in juxtaposition to one another, not as designations that describe any particular thing in and of itself.

In the end, whatever we experience is not dictated or determined by the appearances around us, as is commonly believed. Whether one is attracted by something or repulsed by it, these are only sentiments projected by the mind onto the apparent object. It is the one who is experiencing appearances, the mind, that actually determines what appears to us, as well as determining how we will experience it.

Things do not exist in reality. What we think of as liberation and what we think of as the lower realms are just our thoughts. We definitely experience them as though they were real, and then suffer accordingly. When beings in the hell realms see a burning iron ground, this is nothing but their own thoughts, the hallucination of their defiled minds. This comes about due to the power of ignorance.

When the mind is ignorant of its creative power and so is unable to understand that all creation has its origin within the mind itself, it will often claim that a god or something else has the power to create the things it is experiencing. Alternately, such an ignorant mind may assert that everything is the creation of material elements, of the compounding of different elements together. These are eternalist views.

In this way, those who are blind to the mind's inherent creativity will always attribute responsibility for their own experiences and perceptions to something outside of themselves. Whatever they may perceive, everything, whether tangible or intangible, will be seen as external to or other than themselves. In the same way, what is the point of wearing oneself out by seeking the causes of creation externally or seeking some "other" creator and so wasting valuable time?

Instead, to begin, you should look within and withdraw your mind from its engagement with all these apparent external phenomena. As the mind ceases to focus on an outside world, you can discover that the world that you have been so involved with has actually been outwardly projected by this very mind. As the mind withdraws its projections and beliefs, the world will cease to manifest in the way that it has. This is so because it is only mind that is manifesting the world around us.

This tells us that if we are experiencing happiness, this is the result of wholesome thoughts that we have given rise to in the past. There is no doubt that happy experiences are the manifest expression of virtuous thoughts. These are what create happiness. If we are experiencing unhappiness, it is because our previous unwholesome thoughts have ripened into our present experience of suffering.

While people rightly fear the torments of conditioned existence such as birth in the realms of hell, the teachings of the Buddha do not regard these realms as material, as physically existing. Due to the delusion produced through hatred and negativity, the mind afflicted by anger will experience hell wherever it goes. For one whose mind is filled with aggression, hell is never far away. Hell is an angry state of the mind, which in turn conjures corresponding images — the appearances of the hell realms. It is the same with all the appearances of all the realms of existence, created as they are by their corresponding thoughts and emotions.

One who discovers the key point that mind is the cause of all problems and all solutions learns to unlock, to disentangle, all things associated with the mind. In the end, one finds no other culprit. Mind is the perpetrator of everything that happens, the projector of everything that manifests. Pleasant or unpleasant, whether we go up into higher rebirth or down to the lower realms, whatever we experience is the result of our own mental state. Realizing this, we should no longer grasp at any perception or conception that might arise toward seemingly real phenomena.

Buddha himself has stated in the sutras that all things are only mind. Through realizing this, you will be able to enter and remain in the meditative equipoise of the true nature of mind. If all things are mind, we must look into the nature of this mind. Rather than falling into such extremes as eternalism or nihilism, "being" or "non-being," we should uphold and sustain the genuine view, the true nature of mind.

As a final point, it is said that to realize that all the suffering of samsara is created by our own perception, that heaven and hell are actually states of mind, is very good for the improvement of our view, our understanding of the nature of reality. However, it can be harmful for our sense of renunciation. We should reflect on this accordingly.

> *Up to this point, having shown the stages of the path common to the Bodhisattva Vijñanavada (Mind Only) school, now the uncommon path of the Mahayana Madhyamaka school will be explained.*

> Appearances are of the nature of magical illusions,
> Arising through interdependence.
> Not knowing how to describe their natural state,
> Be joyful in the ineffable.

What we have discussed so far is that there is neither sentient being nor buddha other than one's own precious mind. This truth is emphasized by the teachings of the Mind Only school of Buddhism, which states that all things are only mind. Does this mean that we can leave the matter there, with the conclusion that all things are nothing but mind?

In fact, this is not sufficient. Thus, we are directed to the viewpoint of the Madhyamaka, or Middle Way, school. However, unless you correctly establish at the outset that all things are mind only, you will have no basis upon which to ascertain anything further. Once you have really established that everything you are experiencing is your own mind, then it becomes possible to further discern the reality of emptiness. Thus the knowledge that all is mind is a steppingstone on the way to complete understanding. The view of Mind Only is not the final truth of the Sakya school; it is only a stage that leads one to the enlightened view.

Another important steppingstone to the genuine view is calm abiding meditation (*shamatha*). By learning how to calm the mind and pacify agitated thinking, one is led to the state of clear insight (*vipas-yana*). It is the dawning of the correct view of clear insight that allows us to realize the true nature of mind. However, this state of insight needs to be based on the ability of the mind to abide in tranquility.

Allowing the mind to remain at ease enables us to progress in real-izing the nature of relative truth, which we have been discussing according to the Chittamatra, school and which corresponds with the general or conventional Mahayana view. This understanding can actu-ally enhance one's realization of the Middle Way viewpoint of the Mad-hyamaka school, on the basis of which one will realize the true nature of all phenomena.

Calm abiding meditation is the necessary foundation upon which clear insight may be developed. The more firm and stable is one's prac-tice of calm abiding meditation, the more clear and lucid will be one's realization of insight. Based on a firm and stable calm abiding prac-tice, the clear insight discerning the emptiness of self and other grows more brilliant. This is what is known as the union of calm abiding and clear insight.

While we have mentioned the importance of calm abiding medita-tion, what we are really concerned with here is to be able to recognize the true nature of mind. Let us consider this in terms of the dawning of clear insight in meditation practice. On the subject of how insight unfolds through the process of meditation, there are in the Buddhist tradition a number of approaches, and commentaries on these have been given by many great teachers. In general, a majority of teachers have preferred to rely on the gradual method of progressive insight as the means of guiding their students.

In this approach, one progressively discovers and comes to experi-ence all appearances as mind. Next, all that appears in the mind is found to be illusory. Third, one is then able to understand that these illusory phenomena come about through dependent origination (*ten-drel*). And finally, the nature of dependent origination is realized to be inexpressible. It is to help ensure a clearer realization of insight that so many teachers have chosen to guide students through these four stages of understanding.

This gradual method of developing insight, which begins with the ability to discern all appearances as mind, is explained in detail in the

Lamdre teachings of the Sakya school. The Path with the Result contains the view and teachings expounded by the Indian *mahasiddha*, or "supremely accomplished one," known as Virupa. Some people have occasionally alleged that Virupa was an exponent of the Chittamatra school of Buddhist philosophy. But how could an enlightened *mahasiddha* hold the view of a Chittamatrin? In order to guide others along the path, Virupa explained and taught the Mind Only view prior to his gaining the realization of a *mahasiddha*.

The significance of the Mind Only view is highlighted in the works of Ju Mipham, one of the premier scholars of recent times in the Nyingma school of Tibetan Buddhism. Mipham has stated quite explicitly that to arrive at the Chittamatra view that all is mind is an excellent sign of progress in one's thinking as one's understanding of the Buddha's teaching evolves. But of course he did not leave the matter there but said that it is indeed necessary to progress beyond this stage of understanding.

As we begin our discussion of the Madhyamaka, or Middle Way, view, there is a final point on this topic of mind creating our experience that we must be careful of. If we come to understand that everything is the mind, and yet our mind still seems incapable of projecting anything but more negative experiences, there is a danger that self-doubt, and even self-loathing and self-hatred, might develop as a result.

In order to avoid this possible consequence, it is very important to understand that regardless of the kinds of experiences and appearances the mind projects, they are not real and they are not true. They are like magical illusions produced by a conjuror. Having confidence in this will make things much easier for us, since if we realize that everything is a projection of our own mind and yet is an illusion, this means that all we have to do in order to transform our experience is to transform our mind. We do not leave matters at the understanding that all is mind; we must develop insight into the illusory nature of experience.

Along these lines, Drakpa Gyaltsen is leading us to ask ourselves why, if it is true that all is mind, do appearances assume the forms they do? Why do they not assume the forms and conditions we would prefer to choose for them, if they are the manifestation of our minds? It is out of this line of questioning that the next essential insight evolves, namely that all these mind-created appearances are illusions that come about through causes and conditions.

With the basis or preliminary step of learning to rest your mind in the meditation of calm abiding, from this state you enter the meditation of clear insight. Once we have discovered that everything that appears to us is mind, then as we begin to examine the mind for ourselves in our meditation practice, we discover that it really is like an illusion. Left unexamined, everything seems real enough. But upon closer scrutiny, as we will see, whatever appears doesn't really exist. These illusions our mind displays come about through causes and conditions, through dependent origination, and so do not exist on their own, in their own right.

In order to understand our ordinary dualistic mind (*sem*), one example often used is that of a dream. One may dream of being a king and wielding great power over others, but this only happens in the dream, not in reality. Just like the nature of the dream, whatever occurs in the mind and appears to the mind is illusory. In a dream, whether we become wealthy or poor or whatever we experience, we only seem to go through these experiences because we are afflicted by sleep. None of the dream experiences actually take place; it is only sleep that makes it seem as though they are really happening. We need to meditate well on the example of the dream.

A person afflicted by sleep undergoes dreams that seem to be real although they are not. It is no different with our present waking experience, afflicted as we are by the sleep of ignorance. Through the analogy of sleep and dream, we can understand that the only reason we perceive and experience things the way we do is that we are deluded by ignorance. It is due to ignorance that we are unable to perceive things as they really are. Due to ignorance, our mental and emotional defilements act in conjunction with our accumulated karmic deeds, creating the distorted vision we hold at present regarding ourselves and our world. Thus, all waking experiences in everyday life are distorted by our karma and obscurations.

Everything is a reflection of mind or consciousness. Nothing whatsoever exists other than what appears to the mind due to karma and due to the defilements, the concepts and afflictive emotions. Our karma and defilements create a background upon which our waking life manifests, just as the condition of sleep provides a backdrop for dreams. Without these, we would definitely not experience things in the way we currently do.

Just as when sleeping we perceive dreams as real, so, too, in ignorance we perceive whatever we experience as being real, though it is no more real than a dream. Just as the affliction of sleep causes dreams to seem real to us, so does the affliction of ignorance, our defilements and obscurations, cause our waking life to seem real to us. Just as the condition of sleep makes our nighttime dreams seem real to us, so do our conventional designations and concepts seem to validate our daytime waking experience. And yet the great tantric text of the *Vajrapanjara* states that nothing in samsara or nirvana exists outside of the mind itself.

Through inquiring into these examples and analogies in our meditation practice, we can come to realize that our waking life has no more valid existence than our dream life. The dreams we have at night come about due to many causes and conditions, such as events that have occurred throughout the day. These events are remembered as impressions in the mind. When the immediate condition of falling asleep is present, the dream manifests. Once asleep, the daytime impressions, concepts, and conventions flow through the dreaming mind of the sleeper. This shows us that the dream arises due to different causes and conditions.

As soon as one awakens from the dream, there is no tangible trace of the events one was experiencing just moments before. Nothing that seemed to occur in the dream actually took place. It is exactly the same with all of our daytime "waking" experiences, which are in the same way unreal. Although everything may seem quite normal and valid as far as we are concerned, this is only because we have not yet awakened from the dreamlike slumber of ignorance. Until such time as we wake up, we will continue to experience all these illusory phenomena without knowing that none of these really exist.

These are some of the ways in which understanding develops. Through insight gained in meditation, we can discover that all of our day-to-day experiences are manifested by our karmic propensities or tendencies. They are the manifestation of our karma, our previous deeds, and of our defilements, our negativities. There is nothing inherently real about our perceptions.

The sum of our experience is nothing more than our own minds manifesting the distorted vision of conditioned existence. When you finally understand that all experience and all appearances are mind only, as has been stated by the Buddha, then this means that your experiences do not really exist, that none of this is real. This is what we must realize through our own meditation practice. Coming to understand this, why wouldn't we, then, just allow the mind simply to be as it is? In this way you become able to withdraw from being constantly conditioned by illusory experience and can instead simply allow the mind to rest in supreme peace. This means that you come to rest in the true nature of mind itself.

The view of the Madhyamaka school asserts that mind has no inherent existence. It accepts that how things appear to the mind is the result of many conditions, without there being any inherently existing mind to which things appear. Without discerning the truth about the mind, one will not be able to unravel the many questions and conundrums necessary to fully understand the nature of things. This is how it is laid out in the teachings of the Path with the Result in the Hevajra tradition, where the view is not left simply at saying that everything is mind. Rather, if everything is mind, then all these mental appearances are in fact illusory, since they are only being created by our minds through the interdependence of different causes and conditions.

If you are able to realize this through the practice of meditation, then it is possible to unravel all of your confusion regarding the nature of reality. This produces great benefits. Through realizing this, you will be able to dissolve manifest appearances easily, since once the mind deeply accepts the truth, it is able to put a stop to all projections. Instead, one's mind takes full responsibility, knowing that it, the mind, is the creator.

If one's mind is the creator of all that it experiences, one's mind is also responsible for all the illusions it creates. Through this knowledge, our minds can become independent, unconditioned, uninfluenced by the illusionary nature that we had previously perceived as "reality." In truth, the one who has been conditioned by all these mental illusions is the one who has been watching them. In reality, this one is the observer of an illusory, magical display.

Having pondered the example of the dream in order to understand the illusory nature, our next line of meditative enquiry is to consider the example of watching a magician, a skilled illusionist, at work. When one is an observer at a magic show, the magician is in reality only playing with some mundane object or prop. Yet due to keeping his spectators spellbound, in combination with the other elements of his show, he can create an illusory magical display.

A traditional magician might use various articles, such as a stone, a feather, or a tigerskin, and through deception actually delude an audience into seeing things, such as elephants and horses, that are not really present. Magicians might have a mantra or suggestive "spell" or some ploy they make use of to fascinate their audience. Yet if there is no spectator observing the show, the magician is simply manipulating his props to no effect, and no magical illusion is created.

In the same way, whatever we experience appears to us based on a variety of different causes and conditions. This is the next point to realize, through meditation on the example of a magician's show. Only when the particular causes and corresponding conditions meet will there be the manifestation of whatever mundane appearances we happen to be experiencing. It really is like watching a magic show, where the magician or illusionist requires different conditions such as props, the things he must do or say to support the illusion he wants to create, and of course an audience in whose minds to produce the illusion. If even one of these necessary conditions is lacking, then no illusion is created.

Without the presence of causes and conditions, a magical illusion cannot manifest. Similarly, it is only due to specific circumstances that all things appear to exist. In fact, there is nothing even the size of a sesame seed that truly exists. As everything depends on causes and conditions, it is through understanding causes and conditions that we are able to deconstruct appearances. This is how we come to find out for ourselves that things do not actually exist.

All phenomena are merely conditional, they are the result of dependent origination, of interdependent conditions, just like a magician's illusion. If all mentally generated appearances are no different from those conjured by an illusionist, then all these appearances are also no more real than a conjuror's illusions, no matter how convinced we may be of their validity. We need to know appearances to be illusory creations of our minds in order to understand that what we perceive and experience is not real.

How can we be so sure that these illusionist's tricks of the mind do not really exist? By definition, an illusion is something that does not exist. It only seems to be, due to a variety of composite factors, causes and conditions, the interdependence of which produces illusory scenarios that present themselves to our experience. When the conditions meet, the illusory situation manifests. Without the many causes and conditions that create appearances, there is not a single existing phenomenon to be found anywhere. Meditating deeply on the example of a magic show can bring about definite insight into the unreality of our present vision of things.

Thus, we have established that it is a combination of factors that are compounded to produce the appearances we currently experience. For example, we have our sense organs, the sense objects, the concepts and designations we hold in mind, and so on. When these compounded factors interact with one another interdependently, phenomena are produced through dependent origination. Although they are no more than phantoms, they manifest, but only temporarily, due to causes and conditions. This will continue to be the case until we are able to realize that they are dreamlike illusions, phantom appearances.

Throughout the course of our lives, we regard those who treat us well as friends and those who abuse us as foes. Yet regarding other beings as friend or foe is in fact another distorted perception. In reality, what we are experiencing is the imaginary play of our own attachment and aversion, manifesting as benefactors and enemies. These apparent friends and foes are simply more illusions, arising as such through interdependent conditions and circumstances. All objects of our love, and all objects of our disdain, are reflections of, and in, our own minds.

Magical illusions arise from various factors. Perhaps the most central of these is the spectator who is willing to be spellbound. What this means is that one must be able to withdraw from being spellbound or fascinated by the illusory creations of one's mind. Then one will become independent from, no longer identified with, these illusory experiences. If we are able to realize appearances as illusory, we will cease to grasp and fixate upon them as though they were real. This is the key point.

To summarize what we have understood so far: All things are only mind, and mind itself is illusory. All these reflections of the mind do not exist; their very nature is illusory. These illusory appearances do not exist in themselves independently, but rather they simply come about as the product of many different causes and conditions, through interdependence. These illusory experiences depend on causes and conditions, distinct components that together constitute and manifest what we perceive as our "reality."

This is the meaning of the example of the conjuror, one who can manipulate various conditions in order to delude his audience into believing in something that is not really there. Through meditation on these analogies and the truths they illustrate, one will be able to realize the law of dependent origination (*tendrel*). Phenomena are so dependent on factors other than themselves that nothing happens on its own, and nothing functions independently.

In this regard, the great Indian pandita Nagarjuna has explained the Madhyamaka view by saying that things do not arise from themselves, nor from causes other than themselves; and further, that all things do not arise from both themselves and from external causes, nor do they arise from neither, from no causes at all! In this way, Nagarjuna has refuted all four possible scenarios for birth or production. The work of the Indian master Chandrakirti, the *Madhyamakavatara*, goes to great lengths to further repudiate these four notions of "inherent production."

Nagarjuna teaches that if a thing arises from itself, it would be superfluous, since it already is what it is. In other words, if something comes solely from itself, of itself, it would be redundant, since it would have no need to manifest, already being itself. On the other hand, if phenomena only come from somewhere or something other than themselves, then we have again fallen back on the fallacy of everything being created by some "other," which precludes the possibility of liberation. As meditation deepens and insight develops, one begins to see that a great variety of causes and conditions produce phenomena, and this is how one discovers interdependence, the truth of dependent origination. Through this one learns that none of the four possible viewpoints mentioned by Nagarjuna can be found to be conclusively true.

When you consider deeply the meaning of dependent origination, you can observe that as soon as we state anything or assert any point of view, we have once again presented ourselves with fresh causes that only project more mental confusion. Instead, if you are able to avoid asserting any extreme position, you become able to understand and realize the nature of dependent origination. This law of dependent origination is, in the final analysis, simply inexpressible.

These verses of Drakpa Gyaltsen that we have just explained teach the four successive stages of establishing the true nature of mind. They indicate the importance of developing calm abiding meditation as the basis upon which to realize the nature of mind. As we have said, it is with a mind tamed through calm abiding meditation that one is able to develop clear insight. The awakening of insight begins with the four stages of approaching the nature of reality that we have thus far explained.

We should continue to remind ourselves of these four stages we have been discussing: all appearances are nothing but mind; appearances do not exist inherently, but are like illusions; the fact that illusory appearances can manifest is due to dependent origination; and finally, there are no words that can express the real nature of appearances, as they are ineffable. This is how the realization of clear insight evolves gradually out of calm abiding meditation.

As meditation progresses, we begin to understand, and then to realize, the meaning of the view. Anything that is dependent on factors other than itself does not inherently, of itself, exist. Therefore it is illusory, as the nature of illusions is that they do not inherently exist of themselves. As they lack inherent existence, not existing in their own right, this necessarily means that they depend on factors other than themselves. Things appear, but not because they are; things appear because they are not!

For example, these illusory appearances are just like the moon's reflection in water. You cannot see the moon's reflection in the water unless the moon is present in the sky. It is due to causes and conditions other than themselves that things appear to manifest. There is not a single object that can ever be identified that exists independently, and no single, unique factor can be found that has created any object. All these compounded phenomena rely on many factors and depend on circumstances. Appearances are always temporary, short-lived, since they cannot manifest without all the necessary conditions and circumstances being present.

In the initiation ceremonies of Vajrayana Buddhism, this truth of dependent origination is often demonstrated by ringing a bell at a particular moment and asking the disciples from where the sound of the bell originates. The disciples generally respond that it comes from the body of the bell, or from the ringer within the bell, or from the movement of the teacher's hand. Perhaps a few students might actually respond that it comes from their own ears. And yet the audible sound of the bell arises from all of these factors coming together; any one or two of these factors taken in isolation will not produce the ringing sound.

At the time of initiation, the nature of *dharmata* is indicated through the notion of dependent origination, using a variety of examples. A conch shell may be placed on a mirror. This is to illustrate that only when the conch shell is placed over the mirror will a conch appear in the mirror. There is no conch shell inherent in, or intrinsic to, the mirror. When these composite factors, causes and conditions, are present, only then can the mirror reflect the conch shell.

In the same way, whether you have positive thoughts or negative thoughts, they only arise when they arise due to circumstances, not because such thoughts are inherently present, not because they are there by themselves! All things are illusory, arising through causes and conditions, so no words can ever be capable of expressing the actual nature of all these mental phenomena, no matter how we may try to explain them. The nature of things as they are is inexpressible. It is not that they "are," and it is not that they "are not"! Buddha has not tried to give words to that which is inexpressible.

Choosing not to speak rather that to say something, one is nearer to the realization of the ultimate view. The person who reaches this inexpressible state of mind should remain in meditation, without speaking about whatever truth he or she may or may not have realized. To leave the truth unexpressed is the way in which one may come to gain genuine realization, based on the understanding that has developed through the preceding stages of contemplation and meditation. The true nature of things, dependent origination, is beyond any possible expression in words. This is because the true nature of things is

emptiness. The nature of reality is inexpressible emptiness; it can neither be said nor heard. This being so, it is better simply to remain in
this inexpressible state.

> Up to this point, the manner of meditating upon calm abiding med-
> itation [shamatha] has been indirectly indicated, whereas the man-
> ner of meditating on clear insight [vipasyana] has been directly
> shown in the following way: Having systematically established that
> all objective outer appearances are mind made; that [the mind] is
> illusory; that [the illusion] is without an inherent nature of its own;
> and that [the natureless illusion] is interdependent in origin and
> inexpressible, one meditates on the merging [of the mind and its true
> nature of emptiness], the Absolute devoid of all conceptual extremes.

Thus, we are led to the importance of entering the meditation of
the Middle Way (*Madhyamaka*), or Centrist, viewpoint of Buddhist
philosophy, which avoids the two extreme positions. Because no
expression or elaboration can ever do justice to the nature of reality,
no conclusive statements can be made about dependent origination.
But in fact, dependent origination is the intrinsic nature of the mind.
This is because, finally, the truth of dependent origination reveals the
emptiness and clarity of the mind "as it is." If we understand this, we
may come to appreciate the importance of meditation that unifies
calm abiding and clear insight.

This means that one remains in the inexpressible state, looking at
the empty nature of one's own experience. Then, however near to one
these experiences may be, no words are eloquent enough truly to
express them. This is echoed in the tantric texts of the Hevajra tradition, where it says, "It is so near to us that words do not qualify to
describe it." Once you try to use words to describe experience, you have
already distorted the immediate presence that you actually feel at every
moment.

Nonetheless, although this true nature cannot be expressed, it can be
recognized. While the nature of reality is ineffable, this does not mean
that it is non-existent. Something is present, and this can be experienced by anyone. As the *mahasiddha* Tilopa said to his disciple Naropa:
"It is not that there is nothing. There is something, but I cannot tell

you what it is! You must discover it for yourself." This means that it is not a thought you can think, but you can recognize it for yourself.

In Vajrayana Buddhism, the experience of ineffability is skillfully utilized as an opportunity to recognize the true nature of mind. The ineffable experience may come about in any number of ways, such as through the descent of primordial wisdom (*yeshe bab*) that occurs during initiation. It may occur through the master introducing the manifestation of the clear light of mind (*osal*) in the form of deities. Again, through pressing the wave of enjoyment channels in the body, an experience of the ineffable nature may arise.

These are the means and methods used to exemplify the inexpressible state. We can now understand why one finds in Vajrayana Buddhism such a great variety of methods to bring one into the experience of the ineffable. This experience of inexpressibility, produced through such skillful means, is highly valued by the masters as a method of introducing their disciples to the true nature of mind.

Among all possible methods of introduction, the real primordial wisdom (*yeshe*) is best known through Vajrayana initiation. During initiation, when we receive the blessings of the master, this is the introduction to awareness-wisdom. This is the way it has been taught by Sakya Pandita, who says, "My *mahamudra* is not the practice of focusing one-pointedly on the noticing mind. Rather, it is the wisdom that arises at the time of initiation."

Based on the realization of a great teacher and his power of transmitting blessings, if a disciple has a strong connection with that teacher, deep faith and devotion toward him, the transmission of *mahamudra* may indeed occur during initiation. If one has pure conviction and pure devotion, then one is certain to receive the blessings of the lineage. Receiving blessings depends on one's own faith and pure perception rather than solely depending on the teacher.

What is the nature of the blessings transmitted at the time of initiation? During the initiation ceremony, there is the descent of primordial wisdom (*yeshe bab*), also known as the descent of blessings (*chin bab*). When this occurs, some type of experience may certainly arise in the mind of the disciple. At this moment, one's ordinary thinking processes are halted or suspended. One has the clear and definite feeling of having received blessings. This is when the real primordial wisdom is revealed. Now the teacher may admonish the disciple, in the midst of such deeply felt but inexpressible experience, to recognize the true view. This is how the genuine introduction to the nature of mind is given. This is the state one should continue in.

The same process may be repeated through one's own practice of guru yoga. This is a method that is similar to initiation, by which blessings may be received and introduction to the nature of mind may occur. At the point in the guru devotion practice when the lama dissolves into your body and your mind merges with the lama's mind, just remain in the state of emptiness, unified with the teacher. Simply let things be, resting naturally in the state where the teacher and your own mind are inseparable. Merge the visualization of the master with your own self-knowing awareness. Just as one cannot separate water from wetness, as they are always together and cannot be separated, in the same way one rests in unity with the master. When the lama and one's own awareness are inseparably unified, this is the ultimate guru yoga. Through this practice, we can receive the same blessings as during initiation.

This brings us to the final meaning of the teaching on Parting from the Four Attachments. Just as the third line spoken by Manjushri is concerned with relative bodhichitta, this fourth and final line indicates ultimate bodhichitta, the ultimate mind of enlightenment. Finally, we must arrive at the ultimate view, the understanding of the nature of reality as it is. The intrinsic nature of mind is something that we can look into, discern, and clarify.

The very "suchness" nature of our own minds (*dharmata*) is no different from that of the buddhas themselves. The essence of the enlightened state to be discovered in oneself is exactly the same essence as that of a fully enlightened buddha. It is only due to our defilements and obscurations that we have failed to recognize this nature of mind, the original wakefulness of our own natural awareness. If we really recognize the nature of reality, our awareness-wisdom, then whether we speak of what the Nyingma School calls *dzogchen*, or what the followers of the Kagyu call *mahamudra*, or what the Sakya tradition calls *khorde yerme*, the intention is the same. These teachings are all concerned with how to recognize and realize this intrinsic awareness, as it is.

To continue and gain confidence in the correct view, the subtle meanings of the view must be explained. It is important to question further, to acquire a very clear and precise understanding of the authentic view, by receiving instructions from a qualified Dharma master. This is not something everyone can simply attempt without proper guidance and instruction, without transmission from an authentic lineage. This is because, without proper instruction and continued guidance, one may practice the incorrect view and will be unable to attain liberation from samsara, let alone ultimate enlightenment. This must be understood. Otherwise, when speaking about the view, there is the risk that the teacher may incur transgressions that are greater than the benefits the students may gain from hearing these things.

The genuine view is the one that liberates us from all suffering and all conceptuality. Hence, it is necessary from the beginning to understand that if one clings to or fixates upon one's view, the effect will be the opposite of that intended by the teachings; instead of being liberated, one will be bound. As it is impossible to reconcile or balance the two extreme positions, even if one were to try to hold to both the eternalistic position of "it is" and the nihilistic stance of "it isn't," this still would not resolve the matter. Fixations like these keep us from recognizing the view. Is it not much better to remain simply in a state of non-duality?

The genuine view is free of any duality of subject and object. The observer and the observed are not two separate things that one can somehow perceive independently of one another. Rather than conceptual attitudes that adopt one position or another, one needs to rely upon the recognition of one's own awareness-wisdom, the intrinsic nature of one's own mind. This is, of course, more challenging than merely settling for inaccurate views. However, there is no genuine view of reality apart from the nature of one's own mind.

If all things are dependently produced and do not possess any intrinsically existing nature, then what is the ultimate nature of dependent origination? Between the thought that has just passed and the next thought that is yet to arise there is a pause, a space. This gap between the thoughts, is it something that can be apprehended by thought, or is it inexpressible? Is this gap between the thoughts something you have contrived or fabricated, or is it simply as it is? It is necessary first to rest the mind in this gap or space between the last thought and the next.

Drakpa Gyaltsen says in one of his songs that when he searched for his mind, he was unable to identify the mind's arising, abiding, and ceasing, and so he discovered that mind is birthless. Drakpa Gyaltsen realized that from the beginning, mind has always been empty. This is because mind is empty of cause, empty of any seed of birth, and hence empty of any result. If there is no cause for mind, if the cause does not exist, then there is no birth, abiding, and passing away.

Having found mind to be empty of seed or cause, Drakpa Gyaltsen further found that the mind was also empty of abiding or remaining. Outwardly, one can discover that everything that appears to abide externally is actually composite, a chain of interdependent factors. For example, in the case of a tree, there are the roots, the trunk, the branches, leaves, fruits, seeds, and so on. Inwardly, our mind functions according to interdependent factors, the twelve links of dependent origination, as taught by the Buddha. None of these links exist, none of these links abide independently.

Finally, Drakpa Gyaltsen also found no result or fruition of mind. Mind is totally empty. It has no beginning and it has no end. Hence, there is no way for mind or thought to have any result or conclusion, to end up anywhere. In this way, everything really is empty! If we understand all of this clearly through meditation, then the pure view of emptiness can arise from within us. If we do not understand this well, there are possible risks and pitfalls we may face in our practice. Therefore, these points must be correctly understood.

However, analyzing mind's arising, abiding, and ceasing is still another kind of conceptual thinking. While it is very important, focusing continually on the one-pointed search for the mind is still not the real view. One may think one is searching to discover the nature of mind, but all that one may have instead is an unbroken continuum of conceptual thinking! When our ordinary stream of concepts is present, the true nature of mind is still present, but it is covered by so many thoughts and fixations that we are unable to recognize it. Ultimately, this kind of conceptualization is still what is known as grasping, clinging, or fixating (*dzinba*). As Manjushri said to Sachen, "If grasping arises, you do not have the view."

So why do we need to reexamine again and again the arising, abiding, and ceasing of mind? It is because we must establish our minds in emptiness. How will we be able to bring our minds to emptiness? We need to search and investigate as well as analyze. We must discover emptiness for ourselves, through our own intelligence. Once we have understood through outer examples and inner investigation that our mind is empty of arising, abiding, and ceasing, we are able to genuinely recognize awareness (*rigpa*). This is the key point.

The true nature of mind is emptiness beyond expression. If one discovers the nature of mind, there is no doubt that it is empty. There is nothing visible that can be perceived, since it is not of the domain of the senses. It is beyond expression. You cannot display the nature of your mind to others, and it is indescribable. Discovering your own awareness-wisdom, what you discover is certainly inexpressible.

While it is true that even ordinary mind (*sem*) is empty, this mind is not a blank emptiness like physical space. Some feeling, some experiencing is present, and this is known as "consciousness" (*shepa*). Look into your mind. You can discover that there is something present, some presence of experience. This knowing of experience (*shepa*) is the aspect of clarity within the mind. For example, mind possesses remembering and memory (*dranpa*) and an underlying watchful noticing (*shezhin*), a consciousness of what is taking place. This point is discussed well in the explanations of the nature of mind given by Sakya Pandita. These are indications of how we can understand that mind is not like a substantial or inanimate object.

Similarly, the ultimate nature of mind possesses a natural condition (*rang zhin*) of clarity, and this clarity is self-knowing, self-cognizing. This being so, in order to recognize this innate awareness, you must look into your own mind. The state you discover in this way is not a blank dullness that does not know anything. Rather, it is awake and cognizant. It is beyond thought and expression, and yet it is completely aware.

This awareness that is present in the space between two thoughts is the true nature of mind. Sakya Pandita says that this true nature, the clear luminosity of the mind, is present when the last thought has ceased and the next thought has not yet arisen. Without falling into either the eternalist or the nihilist extreme, one can instead simply recognize one's intrinsic nature, as it is. One must then continue on in this state of recognizing the luminosity of the mind. This is expressed perfectly by Sakya Pandita when he says, "When the past thought has ceased and the next thought has not yet arisen, there is an uninterrupted continuity of clear luminosity (osal)."

Let us examine in more depth what is meant by the clarity of the mind. We can observe that although the objects that appear around us do not seem to change so much, this is not true of our mind. Mind can change in an instant into any form. This capacity for transformation, in which we train when we practice tantric meditation and visualization, is the clarity of our mind.

This clarity is not fixed like some solid or substantial object, since it is mutable and can transform into anything. Hence, we understand that it is also empty. Along the same lines, if you examine this clarity, it is not only mutable, it is also not in any way tangible, and this again is the aspect of emptiness. Through this, we discover that the emptiness and the clarity of mind cannot be separated. This empty clarity is thus known as a unity (zung jug). These two aspects, clarity and emptiness, are coemergent, mutually present; one does not arise without the other. This is the meaning of the non-dual unity of clarity and emptiness (sal tong zung jug).

When Sakya Pandita says in his writings that the base, the path, and the fruition are indivisible, he is speaking about the inseparability of samsara and nirvana (khorde yerme). What Sakya Pandita means is that, in his view, there is no samsara that must be abandoned and no nirvana that must be attained. Instead, it is just a matter of transforming our vision, our perception.

Our five sense consciousnesses are like "sub-minds" included within our general consciousness (namshe). In Vajrayana Buddhist meditation, once all the consciousnesses have been transformed through pure vision, it is still necessary to transform the inclusive eighth consciousness, known as the universal ground consciousness (kunzhi namshe). In this way, our ordinary defiled consciousness (namshe) is transformed into primordial wisdom (yeshe). Finally, this transformation occurs simply through recognition.

To genuinely recognize the nature of mind, we must discover the natural presence (rang zhin) of our mind, which is clarity. We must also see for ourselves that this clarity is, in essence, empty. This clarity and its essential emptiness are inseparable; they are indivisibly one. This is also what is known as the inseparability of samsara and nirvana, and it is the indivisibility of all apparent dualities. When primordial wisdom (*yeshe*) is truly recognized, all phenomena are experienced equally, everything is the same. There is no samsara and no nirvana; there is nothing to abandon and nothing to attain.

The phrase "the unity of clarity and emptiness" (*sal tong zung jug*) is a special term for the view favored by the Sakya tradition. If you care to observe your perceptions, you will find that whatever you perceive and whatever you experience is the reflection of these three: clarity, emptiness, and their unity. This is what is meant by the unity of clarity and emptiness, and this is what you must realize. To realize this is to realize the true nature (*dharmata*) of the buddhas. There are some excellent words of Drakpa Gyaltsen that explain that what is meant by "unity" (*zung jug*) is "empty unobstructed clarity." The radiance (*dang*) of this clarity is not obstructed or confined in any way. It is simply the natural condition of emptiness.

There are many similar terms, such as "the unity of appearances and emptiness" (*nang tong zung jug*). Things do appear, but when you examine them in meditation, you discover that they are empty of any inherent existence. Also, we may speak of the unity of sound and emptiness, or "audible" emptiness (*drak tong zung jug*). Everything that we hear, if examined, is found to be empty. In this case, emptiness is discovered and established through hearing sounds, which are not inherently present by themselves.

The Buddhist tantric teachings often speak of "the unity of bliss and emptiness" (*de tong zung jug*). Whatever pleasure, bliss, or happiness you may experience, if you look into its nature, it is also empty. You discover that the blissful experience and emptiness are indivisibly one. Finally, "the unity of awareness and emptiness" (*rig tong zung jug*) indicates that awareness has no tangible existence. Although it cannot be pinpointed in any way, neither is there a nihilistic absence, since you are cognizant of something! Through exploring the meaning of these important terms, we can know for ourselves that all phenomena are indivisible from emptiness.

A point to note is that when learning to recognize the nature of mind, it might seem as though one part of the mind is watching another part of the mind. If it seems to you that there are two minds or viewpoints, a mind that observes and another aspect of the mind that is being observed, this means that there is still a sense of subject and object in your view. If you have this kind of experience, this is still conceptual thinking (*nam tog*).

The luminosity of mind (*osal*) is not within the scope of conceptual thought. When you really recognize the luminosity between two thoughts, there is no watcher, no observer. This is the unified, nondual state in which there is no subject and no object. These two must be merged together within emptiness, like pouring water into water. This is said to be like merging space with space. For example, here we have a vase. Within this vase, there is empty space. Once we break the vase, the space within the vase merges with the space outside the vase, so that they are not separate.

There is an excellent quote from the *Hevajra Tantra* that offers similar analogies for the nature of mind. The *Hevajra Tantra* says:

> This primordial wisdom is extremely subtle,
> Adamantine [vajra], like the sphere of space.
> It is untainted, ultimate, utterly quiescent,
> And you are its father.

One of the meanings of *vajra* is "diamond." A diamond is adamantine, indestructible; whatever attempts to destroy it will itself be destroyed. This famous four-line teaching says that the primordial wisdom (*yeshe*) is like a vajra, or diamond. It cannot be destroyed by thought or damaged by concepts of any kind. This awareness is like the center of space; it cannot be fixed or pinpointed, nor can it be located anywhere.

Awareness may not be so easy for everyone to discover. The quote from the *Hevajra Tantra* says that it is very subtle. How, then, can we recognize it? The tantra says that you are its father. This means that it is up to you whether you recognize it or not. No one can realize the nature of mind for you. Through your practice, you will be able to realize it. This depends on you!

The true nature of reality is free of any kind of mental elaborations. It is free of any contrived activities, free of being fabricated. It is known as "self-knowing primordial wisdom," or "one's natural awareness-wisdom" (*rang rigpai yeshe*). Though it can be indicated, the very instant you try to grasp this awareness or fixate upon it, you have already strayed from the correct view of the nature of mind.

Instead, to have the view, you must be able simply to recognize awareness (*rang rigpai yeshe*) in which all things are empty, including your own mind. Self-knowing primordial wisdom is the essence of mind, and this is what the mind arises from, abides in, and disappears into. Although it may be difficult to describe, it is definitely present within you. If you are able to recognize this natural awareness-wisdom, then this is what is known as having the view. In order to be able to continue in this state, to remain in the view, the essential point is that you do not grasp on to or fixate on the view. As it is said,

> It is not that something exists,
> Since even Buddha himself could not find it.
> It is not nothing,
> Since everything arises.

As we have said, when the last thought has ceased and the next thought has not yet arisen, there is a gap. In this gap your mind is not like a blank space, as there is some experiencing or knowing present. When recognized, this is luminosity (*osal*); it is also known as self-knowing primordial wisdom, or simply as awareness (*rigpa*). This awareness is a non-dual continuity. Though it can be recognized, this wisdom cannot be pinpointed; it is like an echo in space. Whatever occurs or arises within space has the nature of clarity. Whatever we feel and experience, happiness or unhappiness, all of this is our clarity. And yet the very nature of this clarity is empty space (*ying; dhatu*). So whatever arises also has the nature of empty space.

Whether one speaks of *dzogpa chenpo, mahamudra,* or *khorde yerme,* there is nothing beyond just this; there is nothing more to be discovered. Now, once you have recognized awareness (*rigpa*), it is necessary to remain in that state. "Self-knowing primordial wisdom" refers not only to recognizing but also to sustaining the correct view of the nature of mind, as it is. It is not enough simply to recognize, you must continue on in the recognition. In order to be able to do so, you must receive the transmission and guidance of a genuine master and the blessings of an authentic lineage. This continuity in the recognition of awareness is the real meaning of the inseparability of samsara and nirvana; it is the great seal (*mahamudra*); it is the great perfection (*dzogpa chenpo*).

When you have recognized luminosity, then the aspect of stillness or calm abiding (*shamatha*) and the aspect of insight (*vipasyana*) will both be naturally present. Nevertheless, in order to reach this point, it is beneficial to train oneself in the practice of calm abiding meditation. Once you have trained so well in calm abiding that you can no longer be disturbed by outer circumstances, the state of clear insight arising from this will be excellent. When you have gained experience and become accustomed to the recognition of awareness, all aspects of your knowledge will be greatly increased. You will understand many hidden but essential meanings of the Dharma that you did not understand before.

We don't want to talk about it too much, since the nature of mind is, after all, inexpressible! In the Sakya tradition, we call it the inseparability of samsara and nirvana (*khorde yerme*). In the Kagyu school, it is known as the great seal (*mahamudra*). In the Nyingma teachings, it is self-knowing primordial wisdom, or simply the great perfection (*dzogchen*). This is the perfection of the nature of mind, as it is. Whatever name we may give it, this is not the primary concern. What is important is whether or not we recognize it.

Awareness (*rigpa*) is uncreated and is not something that can be contrived or manipulated in any way. In fact, it is free of all effort of any kind. Self-knowing primordial wisdom is completely free of hope and fear. In it there is no fixation upon concepts. Once you have recognized awareness, then when thoughts arise, do not follow after them. If you do, you will be reentering the unbroken stream of conceptual thinking (*nam tog*)! Instead, having recognized, then when a thought arises, do not grasp it. Simply look toward the essence of the thought, and the thought is gone.

This is seeing the true nature of all phenomena, your own natural awareness-wisdom. If, however, you try to leave your mind merely in nothingness and try to hold on to a state that is empty of any thoughts, this is also the wrong view.

As is said,

> If one grasps on to nothingness,
> There is no chance to gain birth in the pure realms.
> If one grasps on to existence,
> There is no chance to be liberated from samsara.
> So remain in a state that includes both.

In short, your view should be left uncontrived, without fabrication. Your meditation practice should be free of defilements and obscurations, free from distraction and dullness, a well-sustained and disciplined process. Your conduct should be harmlessness to other living beings, kindness and compassion toward others. Untainted by the eight worldly concerns, whatever you do should be simply for the benefit of others.

This completes our commentary on Drakpa Gyaltsen's song of experience based on Manjushri's four-line teaching. Drakpa Gyaltsen concludes his song by dedicating to others whatever merit may be derived from spontaneously expressing this song on Parting from the Four Attachments:

> By the merit of this virtue
> Of explaining the Parting from the Four Attachments,
> May all the seven races of living beings
> Be established upon the stage of buddhahood.

The author concludes with the dedication of merit and indicates the result.

As Jetsun Drakpa Gyaltsen, the great lay practitioner of the Sakyapas, is a fully experienced and realized yogi, he shares this teaching as a pith instruction, an experiential oral instruction, for the sake of all. He dedicates the merit to the enlightenment of all sentient beings.

Normally we do not hear of seven realms as mentioned in the lines of dedication, but rather six realms within the desire realm. The realm that is added here is that of beings dwelling in a state of limbo, or *bardo*, the intermediate state between births. Beings may remain trapped in the *bardo* state, unable to take birth in any of the six realms. The *bardo* beings have passed away from one of the six realms but have not yet found another rebirth. They are caught in an intermediate state, a kind of limbo between the previous life and the next. Drakpa Gyaltsen prays that all of these seven varieties of beings may achieve buddhahood.

Traditionally, this teaching of Parting from the Four Attachments would be given over a period of seven days. If one were to elaborate, it might take two months. It has been a source of great happiness to me to be able to share this with all of you with whom I have a strong spiritual connection. We can all rejoice that the karma we share has allowed us to hear these teachings.

First, we have explained how to discern the proper form of ethical conduct, study, contemplation, and meditation, as well as how to distinguish between authentic and artificial morality, study, contemplation, and meditation. Second, we have explained how to follow a more genuine form of renunciation, while discarding shallow pursuits.

Third, we have shown the necessity of dedicating oneself to the precious bodhichitta, the most prized and genuine form of altruism, for the sake of all sentient beings. We have discussed how to generate bodhichitta on the basis of true love and compassion for others. Fourth, in relation to the correct view of emptiness, we have explained how in order to realize the Middle Way, the true nature of mind, it is essential for us not to fall into any extreme or polarized position, as represented by the two extreme viewpoints. We now dedicate the merit of this activity for the benefit of all sentient beings.

The words of this teaching are concise, yet they contain all the meanings of sutra and tantra. These words spoken by Manjushri to Sachen Kunga Nyingpo are held in great respect by all Buddhist traditions. All the teachings of the Sakya and of the Lamdre, as well as those of the Nyingma and Kagyu, the Kadam and Gelug schools, are contained in these four lines. All of the meanings of Patrul Rinpoche's *Words of My Perfect Teacher* (*Kunzang Lamai Shelung*) are contained herein. Everything is an elaboration on these few lines.

Although this teaching of Parting from the Four Attachments is only four lines long, if you ponder deeply the meanings contained in them, you will discover for yourself that the essential meaning of all the sutras and tantras is present. These precious four lines should be memorized.

I will offer my prayers that their blessings may enter your mindstreams and remain there.

I am an ordinary person, but the blessings of my spiritual masters have definitely affected me. I hope that whatever blessings I have received will also come to you. May all the meanings of Parting from the Four Attachments become your own realization. This means to be free from attachment to this life, free from attachment to worldly existence, free from attachment to selfish purposes, and free from attachment in the view.

Appendix 1: Prayer to the Lineage Gurus of "Parting from the Four Attachments"

by Ngorchen Kunga Zangpo

The teacher of living beings, the fully enlightened one,
The conqueror's chief son, the protector Manjushri, and
The holy Sakyapa (Kunga Nyingpo) who was favored by him,
To these three unequalled, excellent refuges I pray.

Sonam Tsemo who accomplished the five knowledges,
Jetsun Rinpoche (Drakpa Gyaltsen)
who knew all the sutras and tantras, and
Sakya pandita, who was the second lord of sages,
To these three regents of the conqueror I pray.

Phagpa Rinpoche, the owner of the teaching,
Konchok Pal who obtained the wealth of the tantras
Through hearing, contemplation, and meditation, and
Choje Takphukpa who gained the excellent attainment,
To these three holy attainers of knowledge I pray.

Sonam Gyaltsen, the crown jewel of living beings,
Palden Tsultrim, the master of instructions,
and Yeshe Gyaltsen, the omniscient one,
To these three teachers and excellent guides I pray.

The omniscient Ewampa (Ngorchen Kunga Zangpo)
Who was prophesied by the conqueror,
His foremost (spiritual) son Konchok Pal, and

Sonam Senge, the sun of speech,
To these three accomplishers of knowledge and liberation I pray.

Sangye Rinchen, the real Manjushri,
Namkha Wangchuk, the great being, and
Kunga Lekdrup, possessor of precepts and learning,
To these three illuminators of the teaching I pray.

Kunga Chodak, the expounder of logic,
Kunga Namgyal, the lord of attainments, and
Tenzin Zangpo, the accomplisher of knowledge,
To these three holy guides I pray.

Ngawang Lhundrup who obtained knowledge and attainment,
Morchen Je, the all-seeing sun of the Dharma, and
Nesarwa, the source of the ocean of instructions,
To these three incomparable teachers I pray.

Kunga Lodro, the life-force of the teachings
In these degenerate times,
Chime Tenpa'i Nyima, the holy one, and
Dorje Rinchen, the youthful Manjushri,
To these three excellent guides of living beings I pray.

Kunga Tenzin, the owner of the hearing-lineage
Khyentse Wangpo who attained the level of Manjushri,
and Loter Wangpo who was favored by him,
To these three protectors of the teaching and living beings, I pray.

Tenpa'i Wang, famed for possessing
The splendor of loving kindness,
Chokyi Nyima, the son of the Victorious One, and
Zhenphen Nyingpo, the great treasure of compassion,
To these three unequalled sons of the conquerors I pray.

By this prayer to the collection of holy teachers,
May they swiftly look upon me with the eye of compassion

And bless me to sincerely turn away from
Attachment to the appearances of this life,
Which is the very basis for destruction.

Bless me to give rise to a powerful renunciation
For these three realms of constant torment,
Where distressful sufferings are so unbearable
And where there is no chance for even a little happiness.

Having meditated well, for the purpose of living beings
Who have been my mothers,
On the thought of enlightenment
Which equates and exchanges self and others,
The only path traversed by the conquerors and their sons,
Bless me to part from fancying my own purpose.

Though appearing, all phenomena from the beginning
Are like a dream and a magical illusion.
Having determined these to be empty and without truth,
Bless me to produce within my mind the pure middle path
The non-dual state that is completely devoid of
Grasping at any extreme.

Having proceeded toward the Dharma,
Traversed the path of the Dharma,
And dispelled individualistic errors of the path
Through meditating in this way,
Bless me that illusory visions appear
As the great primordial wisdom of tire enlightened ones.

(This prayer to the lineage Gurus of the instructions for Parting from the Four attachments was written by the Sakya monk Kunga Zangpo at Sakya.)

Translated by His Holiness Sakya Trizin and Jay Goldberg

Appendix 2: Tibetan Text of Drakpa Gyaltsen's Song

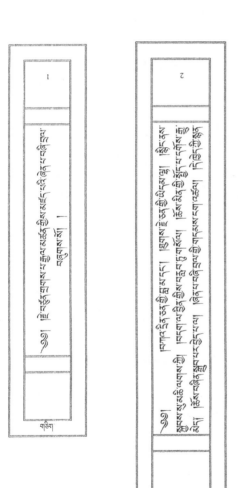

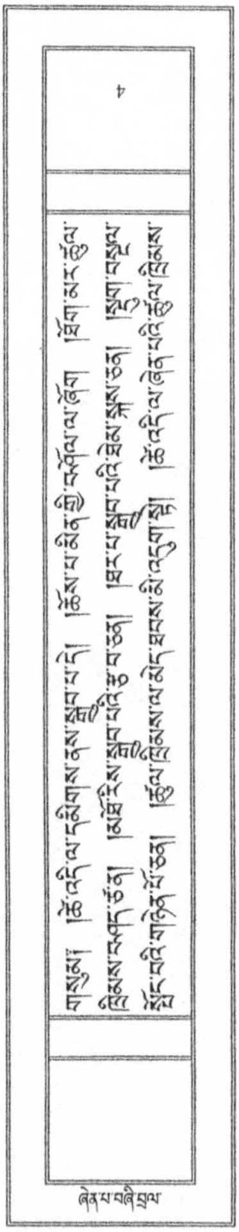

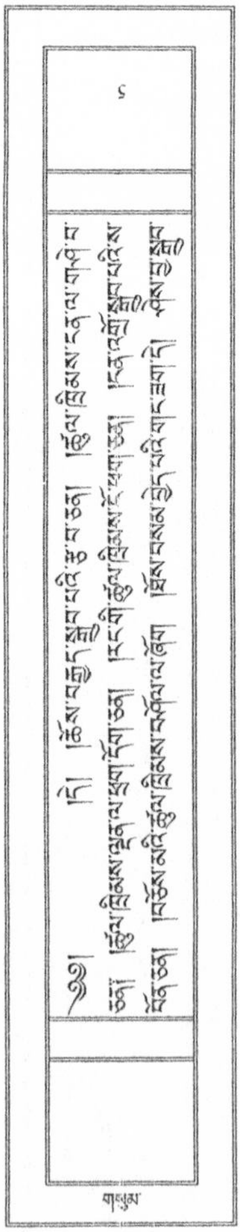

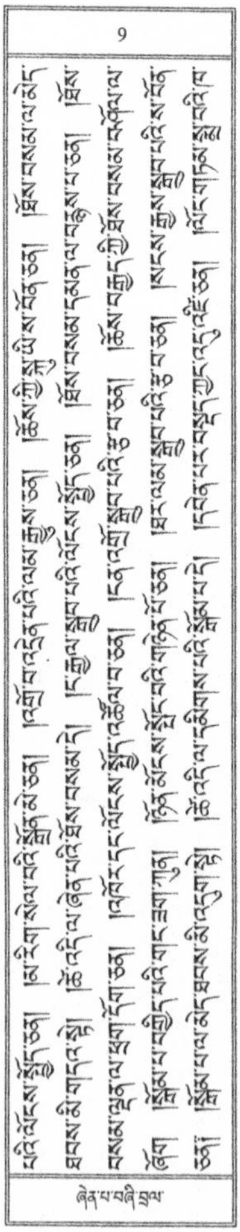

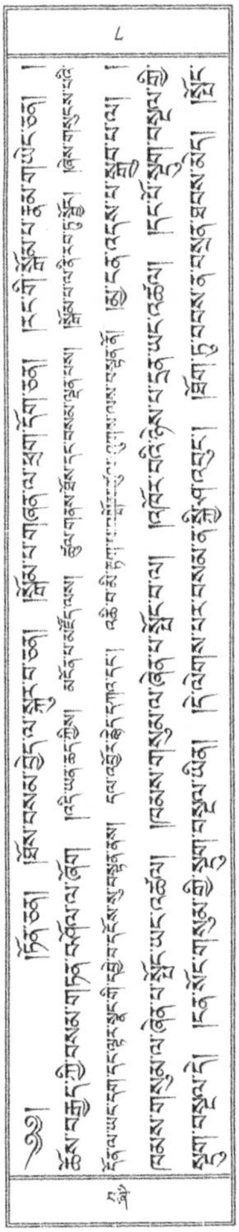

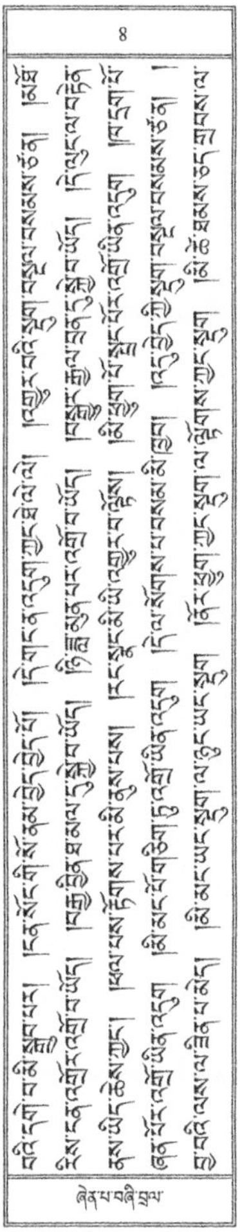

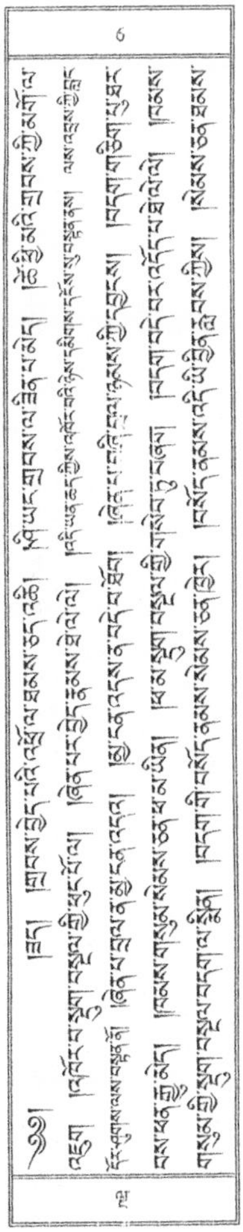

ཞེན་པ་བཞི་བྲལ

10

ཅན་སངས་རྒྱས་ཤོག །འདི་ཡན་ཆད་ཀྱིས་རྒྱུ་བྱམས་པ་དང་སྙིང་རྗེ་བསྒོམ་པ་ཤུགས་ལས་བསྟན་ནས། འབྲས་བུ་བདག་གཞན་བརྗེ་བ་དངོས་སུ་བསྟན་ཏོ། །བདག་ཏེ་ལྟར་འདུག་ཀྱང་
ཆོས་ཉིད་ཀྱི་དང་། །འཛིན་དང་བཅས་ལ་གྲོལ་བ་མེད། །དེ་ཡང་ཞིབ་ཏུ་དཔྱད་ཙ་ན། །ཡོད་པར་འཛིན་ལ་ཐར་པ་མེད། །མེད་པར་འཛིན་ལ་མཐོ་
རིས་མེད། །གཉིས་ཀར་འཛིན་པ་མི་ཤེས་པས། །གཉིས་མེད་ཀྱི་ངང་ལ་གང་དགར་ཞོག །འདི་ཡན་ཆད་ཀྱིས་རྟག་ཆད་ཀྱི་ལྟ་བ་སྤངས་ནས་ཟུང་འཇུག་གཉིས་མེད་ལ་
བློ་འདོག་ཚུལ་སྦྱོར་བསྟན་ཏོ། །ཆོས་ཀུན་སེམས་ཀྱི་སྤྱོད་ཡུལ་ཡིན། །ཕྱུ་དང་དབང་ཕྱུག་ལ་སོགས་པ། །འབྱུང་བཞིའི་བྱེད་མཁན་མ་འཚོལ་བར། །
སེམས་ཉིད་ཀྱི་ངང་ལ་གང་དགར་ཞོག །འདི་ཡན་ཆད་ཀྱིས་བྱང་སེམས་སེམས་ཙམ་པ་དང་ཐུན་མོང་བའི་ལམ་རིམ་བསྟན་ནས། ཐེག་ཆེན་དབུ་མ་པའི་ཐུན་མོང་མ་ཡིན་པའི་ལམ

དཀ་ཚོམ།

11

༄༅། །ཞི། སྣང་བ་སྒྱུ་མའི་རང་བཞིན་དང་། །རྟེན་ཅིང་འབྲེལ་བར་འབྱུང་བ་ཡི། །གནས་ལུགས་བརྗོད་པར་མི་ཤེས་ཀྱི། །
བརྗོད་བྲལ་གྱི་ངང་ལ་གང་དགར་ཞོག །འདི་ཡན་ཆད་ཀྱིས་ཞི་གནས་བསྒོམ་ཚུལ་ཤུགས་ལས་བསྟན་ནས། ལྷག་མཐོང་བསྒོམ་ཚུལ་ལ། ཡུལ་སྣང་སེམས་སུ་བསྒྲུབ་པ་དང་། དེ་སྒྱུ
མར་བསྒྲུབ་པ་དང་། དེ་རང་བཞིན་མེད་པ། རྟེན་འབྲེལ་དང་། བརྗོད་བྲལ་དུ་གཏན་ལ་ཕབ་ནས་སྤྲོས་བྲལ་ཟུང་འཇུག་བསྒོམ་པ་དངོས་སུ་བསྟན་ཏོ། །ཞེན་པ་བཞི་བྲལ་ཕྱེད་པ་ཡི། །
དགེ་བ་འདི་ཡི་བསོད་ནམས་ཀྱིས། །འགྲོ་བ་བདུན་པོ་མ་ལུས་པ། །སངས་རྒྱས་ས་ལ་འགོད་པར་ཤོག །འདིས་བསྔོ་བ་དང་། འབྲས་བུ་བསྟན་ཏོ། །ཞེན་པ
བཞི་བྲལ་གྱི་གདམས་ངག རྣལ་འབྱོར་པ་གྲགས་པ་རྒྱལ་མཚན་གྱིས་དཔལ་ས་སྐྱའི་དགོན་པར་སྦྱར་བའོ།།

Made in the USA
Las Vegas, NV
29 December 2021

39802081R00121